All You Need is Luck

All You Need is Luck

When the kids left home, so did they.
The hilarious adventures of a couple who
made world travel a way of life.

Frank Nelson

Writers Club Press
San Jose New York Lincoln Shanghai

All You Need is Luck
When the kids left home, so did they.
The hilarious adventures of a couple who made world travel a way of life.

Writers Club Press
an imprint of iUniverse, Inc.

For information address:
iUniverse, Inc.
5220 S. 16th St., Suite 200
Lincoln, NE 68512
www.iuniverse.com

ISBN: 0-595-22668-X

Printed in the United States of America

For Maria

.

Contents

Introduction 1

YEAR ONE

CHAPTER 1 7

CHAPTER 2 25

CHAPTER 3 45

CHAPTER 4 61

CHAPTER 5 81

YEAR TWO

CHAPTER 6 99

CHAPTER 7 115

CHAPTER 8 129

CHAPTER 9 143

CHAPTER 10 161

CHAPTER 11 181

Introduction

Watching the runway blur beneath the wheels of our tiny aircraft as we left Blenheim, at the northern tip of New Zealand's South Island, I was reminded again just how fast everything was happening. This small town had been our home for the past 12 years and after what seemed only a few short weeks of planning, we were leaving everything behind. So many friends and familiar places, to say nothing of our house and, by far the biggest wrench of all, Buffy, our golden retriever. Oh, and did I mention, our jobs, pension schemes and all those other security trappings we'd spent 20 years telling our children were important and they needed to start planning for?

A group of close friends came to the airport to see us on our way with a typically madcap mix of cheerful but tearful goodbye songs, jokes and ribald last-minute advice for the unwary traveller. Less than an hour before we had locked the last of the possessions we were leaving behind in one room of our rambling old house, said hello and goodbye to our new tenants, taken photos of the house and garden and left everything in the hands of Bob Boyes, a man we lightheartedly dubbed our "property manager". Misty eyed and feeling highly emotional, we popped across our small paddock to the next door neighbours, taking Buffy and all his paraphernalia. He was 11 then and though we knew we'd see him again, we didn't know if he would even recognise us in seven dog year's time. We drove our ancient Ford Cortina estate the few miles to the airport and left it there with a "For Sale" sign in the window. We had been trying unsuccessfully to sell it for some time and this was a final throw of the dice with Bob agreeing to handle things from this point. It wasn't a bad car and was certainly cheap enough but it was still almost five months before Bob was able to clinch the deal with a couple of German backpackers.

1

Crammed into our seats aboard what the locals liked to refer to as White Knuckle Airways, with bits of bunting still clinging to our hair and clothes, we blinked back tears as the plane wheeled away from the terminal. As if it wasn't quite sure what to do, the plane bucked and weaved uncertainly along the tarmac before making up its mind and springing skywards. Suddenly we were airborne with vineyards and orchards spreading out in all directions, Blenheim's colourful roofs beneath us, Cook Strait glistening ahead and beyond that across the water New Zealand's capital city, Wellington. The flight takes only about 20 minutes and for almost the whole way my wife and I sat in silence, each of us in the grip of the same bowel-churning thought: "What the f*** are we doing?"

At a time when many people our age—I was 48 and Maria 44—were concerned about basic job security as much as career prospects, we had blithely given up two excellent, well paid jobs. I left the local newspaper, where I was deputy editor and senior reporter, while Maria, a registered nurse, resigned from the accident and emergency department of the Blenheim area hospital. And just when contemporaries were starting to get serious about calculating retirement benefits and insurance policy payouts, we cashed in all ours, using the proceeds to paint the house and buy a couple of round-the-world air tickets. After years of chanting the mantra of responsibility to the kids, we had become totally irresponsible…

Of course, I knew something was up. For one thing, my wife rarely came into the newspaper office where I worked, well not at three o'clock in the afternoon, and definitely not to invite me out for coffee. Another giveaway was the 10-pound World Atlas tucked casually under one arm, giving her a curiously lopsided gait. The cafe we chose was virtually empty, so we took our drinks to one of the largest tables where Maria immediately flipped open the atlas at North America. Bubbling over with excitement, her finger fled to the top right hand corner of that vast land. "How do you fancy Vermont?" I gently pushed her index finger to one side, revealing a speck on green labeled

"V'mont", an American state obviously so small the map-maker could not even find room for the full name. "Sounds great!" I said. And I really meant it. A letter in Maria's pocket had brought a job offer from an American summer camp that was to be the first step along the path of our new adventure, the jumping off point which would snap the last of our suburban chains. We now had work waiting for us in Vermont in June, then jobs lined up in England for September and October. After that we planned to spend six months in Melbourne where we were confident something else would turn up.

Once our tiny plane landed in Wellington we transferred to a Qantas jumbo bound for Sydney. But not just yet—a technical fault meant we all sat there sipping orange juice for two hours before being unloaded. We changed planes and flew north to Auckland, New Zealand's largest city, where Qantas installed us in a hotel and gave us dinner and breakfast. We ate our first breakfast of the day in our room at 5.15 next morning, caught the airport shuttle bus and were soon tightening our seat belts for Australia. Breakfast number two was served on the way to Sydney where we connected with a flight to Hawaii. Our third breakfast arrived 30,000 feet above the Pacific as we hurtled towards Honolulu. Lunch and dinner followed on this nine-hour flight which gave us plenty of time to reflect on what we were doing. Lots of nagging doubts still persisted but we patted their heads by reminding ourselves we were only going to be away for a year initially. The longer term plan might stretch to two years of travelling provided we stayed healthy, could find jobs as we went, the house remained rented, our finances kept on an even keel and 101 other things went our way. In any case, as we kept telling ourselves and everybody else: "If things don't work out, we can always come home."

Six years later we're still going, still circling the globe, working primarily in the United States, Australia and England and having a fantastic time. Somehow we've been lucky enough to step outside the confines of regular jobs and the host of other commitments which keep most people pinned down for so much of their lives. Of course we know the magical lifestyle we've stumbled into is not reality. One day we'll rejoin the real world, go back to Blenheim and resume enjoying that lovely, irreplaceable sense of being part of a community again. But until then...

YEAR ONE

○ ○

"Terrible tragedy in the South Seas. Three million people trapped alive!"

—Tom Scott, New Zealand humourist

1

People always joke about New Zealand, about how quiet and empty it is, that there's almost no traffic and how the relatively few people are heavily outnumbered by many millions of sheep. I think it was Scottish comedian Billy Connolly who quipped that he went to New Zealand but it was closed! We emigrated there from England in 1979 with our two children, then aged three and four. A gruelling 30-hour journey brought us from London's Heathrow airport to this tiny outcrop of the British Empire, the two main islands barely 1,000 miles long between them, little more than a speck in the South Pacific. New Zealand's biggest advantage, and at the same time it's biggest disadvantage, is its geographical position and isolation. Australia is three hours flying away and several smaller Pacific islands, such as Fiji and Tonga, are within similar range. But England and the rest of Europe, and the United States, are some serious distance away in terms of both miles and money.

Looking back 20-odd years to when we first arrived, it certainly seemed a sleepy little slice of paradise, clean and green, warm and sunny, and safe. Above all, the standard of living was high and the cost of living low: quite simply, New Zealand offered a lifestyle we could never have afforded had we stayed in England. By the time we started travelling in 1996 all those things were still true but perhaps a little less so. Over the course of almost two decades New Zealand has inevitably caught up with the rest of the world or the outside world has caught up with New Zealand. One result is that the pace of life there has quickened considerably even though it may still be only a sedate trot compared to the flat out gallop of, say, London or Los Angeles.

Almost as soon as we left New Zealand, we noticed a strange thing happening...time started to go very much more slowly. After the burly-burly and pressure of working often very long hours in two demanding jobs, we suddenly had an excess of that luxury commodity, time. This in turn gave rise to another strange sensation—for a long while, probably for most of our first 12 months on the road, it felt as if we were on holiday even though we were working. According to the old saying, a change is a good as a rest, and we were now on course for plenty of changes. Perhaps that partly explains why something of the holiday feeling still survives even after six years of wandering the world.

We said farewell to New Zealand on a frosty morning in early June 1996 and it no doubt helped ease our homesickness that we spent our first week in the toasty, tropical paradise of Hawaii. We whiled away the time just soaking up some sunshine, splashing in the warm waters off Waikiki and walking along the beach at night. Hotels and restaurants right on the ocean spiked the sand with flaming torches and the air was heady with the scent of jasmine, frangipani, salt spray and Big Macs. We went to the obligatory dance show at one of the large hotels where I was relieved not to have been among those unfortunates plucked from the audience to demonstrate, with all the grace of a rheumatoid rhinoceros, my abysmal lack of hula skills. We also took an island tour around Oahu which included stops to admire the scenic highlights and to taste fresh pineapples and macadamia nuts. Davis, our guide, had worked as a driver on about a dozen films and pointed out locations used for such sandy television series as *Hawaii Five-O* and *Magnum PI*, and for the movie *Jurassic Park*.

Before setting out on this adventure we had equipped ourselves with two heavy-duty cases which converted into backpacks and taken out senior membership of the Youth Hostel Association. The word "youth" triggered all sorts of merriment and teasing among our friends, but we soon found age was no barrier to hostelling around the world. We have made full use of YHA hostels in several countries and met many people much older than us happily backpacking their way around. Even more surprising is that many of them are travelling for a year or longer, like us making the most of that window of "freedom" between the kids leaving home and the drooling years once the grand-children arrive.

In Waikiki we booked into one such hostel. It was cheap and handy for everything being just a couple of blocks from the beach, but it was also noisy and there was no air conditioning. Even on full power, the single ceiling fan in our room was like a languid soup ladle, just constantly stirring up the hot, sticky air, and though we were dog tired we found it hard to sleep. After three days we persuaded the manager to let us move into the hostel's bungalow at Punaluu, on the north-east coast of the island. Set against the backdrop of the brooding Koolau Range, where forest-covered mountains dissolve into low, smoky rain clouds, this was a beautifully furnished holiday retreat which we were delighted to find we had all to ourselves. We explored the local village, walked and swam our way for miles along the near-deserted beach, and on Sunday went to the tiny whitewashed church of St Joachim.

Though we were both raised as Catholics, the only time we now regularly attend church is at Christmas, and then we generally try to spread our custom around, going to a different one each year. However, travelling is different and there's no doubt that popping into church services, including weddings and funerals, often gives a curious insight into the life of the local community. This was no exception. As a warm breeze reluctantly dragged itself through the open windows and doors, churchgoers, many dressed in dazzlingly colourful dresses and shirts, fanned themselves with hymn sheets. We were all swept along by the beautiful singing of a local choir and towards the end of the service any visitors were invited to identify themselves. There were a few people from neighbouring islands and a couple of Americans before we shyly stood up and said we were from New Zealand. The tiny church went wild, as if we had travelled all the way just for this service, and a lovely woman came forward, kissed us both warmly on the cheek and placed woollen leis around our necks. These were the first of many souvenirs we were to collect on our world travels and they remain among our most treasured.

We flew out of Honolulu just after midnight, changed planes in Los Angeles and arrived in New York around 10pm the next night. We had arranged work in the States, together with the necessary visas, through Bunac, one of several organisations which trawl through New Zealand and Australia for American summer camp staff. As part of the deal we had to attend an orientation in New York where a night's accommodation was arranged for us and hundreds of other camp counsellors. Someone from Bunac was supposed to collect us from the airport. However, when we landed nobody was there and the contact numbers yielded only irritating after-hours messages.

So we caught our first New York cab driven by a recently-arrived Bangladeshi who inexplicably opted for a route taking us through the heart of Harlem. Now this might be a colourful, vibrant, fascinating place to visit by day, but at midnight it looked like a war zone with rows of shops all boarded up, rubbish piled high in doorways and groups of people hanging around on street corners, lurking near traffic lights, flitting in and out of the shadows. Even our driver soon began to look distinctly uneasy, constantly checking the doors were locked and cursing whenever we had to stop at a red light. It was certainly a nerve-jangling introduction to the Big Apple for these Kiwi country mice.

We had another five days in New York, staying in a couple of cheap hotels and spending every day pounding the pavements and just devouring the sights and sounds, the smells and speed, and above all the sheer size and scale of this magnificent city. We did most of the touristy things—a boat ride around Manhattan Island, bus tours uptown, downtown and midtown, Times Square, Fifth Avenue, Central Park, the Stock Exchange, Empire State and Chrysler buildings, Greenwich Village, Little Italy, Chinatown and the World Trade Center. We took in a Broadway show, *Smokey Joe's Cafe*, and at the United Nations, feeling a bit homesick, bought a little New Zealand flag which we "flew" in our room wherever we were staying over the next couple of years. Almost daily we seemed to stumble across a different film being shot somewhere in Manhattan and on one of our bus tours the sassy little Latino guide, perhaps with ambitions towards a movie career, launched into a breathy rendition of *Memories* after discovering two of her passengers were celebrating their golden wedding.

Then there was Donald Trump's 50th birthday bash. Walking along Fifth Avenue we came across a red carpet running from the road-way, over the pavement and through the imposing front entrance of Trump Tower. We joined the crowd gathered there watching limos arrive for what we found out later was Trump's big party. Guests seemed to fall into two distinct categories: those who hurried in heads down, and those who stopped to smile and wave to the curious gallery of onlookers. We didn't recognise many of them but a couple who did stand out were crooner Tony Bennett and actress Morgan Fairchild. Later that night we went up the Empire State Building where, more than 1,000 feet above Manhattan, we were treated to a wonderful fire-works display from Donald's place just down the road. From the top of that most famous of buildings we also tried to ring our daughter back in New Zealand thinking that would be something for the mental scrapbook of memorable moments. But typically she wasn't home!

Perhaps the most vivid lasting impression of New York is the way in which the city's inhabitants have raised rudeness to an art form. We now realise the soup nazi featured in the hit television comedy series *Seinfeld*, is not an entirely fictional character. During a trip to the cut-price ticket booth at the World Trade Center we spent a good hour enjoying the performance of the man behind the desk. If you knew exactly what you wanted he would deign to serve you: otherwise, watch out. He employed a ruthless strategy for dealing with timid tourists who dared ask anything about the storyline of certain shows or how good the views were from particular seats. Chomping on the soggy end of a fat cigar and staring straight over their heads he would simply ignore their questions and bellow "Naaaxt!" On another occasion we bought some cheese and fruit and two bread rolls in a street corner deli. The whole lot were unceremoniously plonked on the counter in front of us by an unsmiling owner when we made the mistake of asking if he could butter our rolls for us. His face didn't change one iota as he snatched them back, hacked them open, smeared two butter pats inside and slammed them back down again with a force which flattened them. We just burst out laughing and stumbled from the shop helplessly clutching our sides. You had to hand it to these people…they were real pros.

By now we were due to head for our summer camp so, armed with a bulky copy of the *New York Times* to while away the 10-hour bus trip, we set off for Vermont. There are something like 10,000 summer camps sprinkled throughout the United States. There are camps for the very rich, where kids arrive by helicopter, glued to mobile phones and laden down with designer clothes; there are camps for kids from inner city ghettos who arrive with nothing but a lot of attitude; there are camps for the fat and the thin, for children, for adults, for families, for under-achievers and over-achievers, for sports freaks and computer nerds, for all sorts of specialist pursuits or hobbies—in short, camps for just about anyone and anything. With such a range of camps and spectacular locations to choose from, we were to look back later and consider our first experience of this great American institution a little unlucky.

It was dusk when Judy, our camp director, met the bus in the small Vermont town of Newport and drove us off into the wilderness to the camp nestled in pine trees only a few miles from the Canadian border. In the gathering gloom, our first glimpse of the camp was through shimmering clouds of mosquitoes which proved to be among many problems we were to encounter. Every morning we virtually had to bathe in insect repellent to keep them at bay, and some of our fellow counsellors, especially the tender young ones fresh from England, suffered terribly. Maria, as camp nurse, had to deal with this bumpy legacy of bites and stings, along with a host of other mainly minor ailments. Most of our fellow counsellors were American and ex-campers themselves, quite a few were English while others came from France, Ireland, Italy and Slovenia. There were about two dozen of them and what a great bunch, average age around 20, with tons of energy and enthusiasm which they doubtless needed. As we all very soon found out, the kids were hard work and some long, demanding days lay ahead.

The youngsters were mainly from economically and socially disadvantaged backgrounds and an unsettling number came with sad little histories of physical or sexual abuse. Some who lived locally were dropped off early in the morning and picked up again late afternoon. Others came maybe for a week or a fortnight while a few poor souls were simply dumped there for the whole summer by parents who thought they had better things to do than spend time with their children. My official title was "day camp director" and with the help of two young local women my job was to organise and run activities for up to about 30 kids ranging in age from eight to 15. My assistants were as different as chalk and cheese and I secretly named them accordingly.

One was about 24, wore braces and no-nonsense denim dungarees, was very sensible and full of bright ideas; the other was a budding bimbo who dressed like Barbie at the beach, was constantly sipping coffee from a plastic mug, and spent hours at home sticking on the most vivid false fingernails. Each morning she would flounce in and show off her handiwork from the previous evening. Holding up her hands in front of her face she would peer through a forest of maybe 10 little American flags, 10 smiley faces, 10 snowflakes or 10 of some other colourful design. She always wanted to know what I thought of her latest bizarre fashion statement and it wasn't long before I mastered the perfect response. Borrowing one of her most over-used expressions I would restrict myself to the simple yet noncommittal verdict: "Whatever". She was a cheerful enough girl but tended to spend much more time planning her hectic social life than organising less amorous activities such as softball games, nature rambles or art classes for the kids.

Ours was a small camp compared to most, catering for a maximum of around 100 children at any one time. Before the first of them set foot in the camp we underwent a week of staff training and familiarisation. This included theory sessions covering everything from first aid, CPR and recognising sexual abuse, to a visit by a rotund gentleman whose name tag proclaimed him to be a genuine "Bear Warden". Maria and I were enthralled by his tales of black bears and bobcats, porcupines and possums, moose, raccoons and skunks, and excited to be sharing the same territory as such exotic creatures. We were desperate to see bears and amid the welter of questions at the end of the talk on the best ways of avoiding contact, two English voices could clearly be heard politely inquiring where would be the best place to actually encounter these magnificent animals.

The warden, unsure if he was the butt of some tasteless British humour, fixed us with a baleful stare and announced solemnly and slowly, as if talking to a couple of remedial village idiots, "You don't wanna tangle with them critters." Beginning to feel as if we were slipping into a *Monty Python* sketch we explained we certainly didn't want to tangle with anything, least of all 800 pounds of morose teddy, but we would be very grateful if he could tell us the best place to go in the hope of seeing bears. His response this time neatly brought the debate full circle: "No siree, you don't wanna tangle with them critters." To our intense disappointment, the only wildlife we came across in Vermont were a few squirrels, some groundhogs and, most memorably, a snake which was sunning itself contentedly until one of the kids, apparently not a nature enthusiast, threw a Coke bottle at it.

That same training week gave counsellors a chance to concentrate on their specialist areas such as canoeing, sailing, archery, riflery and ropes. The term "specialist areas" was perhaps overstating things just a bit. For example, the people assigned to run the archery, far from being a merry band of potential Robin Hoods, were all raw novices whose "expertise" was mysteriously gained in the few hours between leaving the camp just after lunch one day and turning up again at dinner time. Similarly, a late arrival to the camp staff, whose speciality was ballet and modern dance, was surprised to find herself spending the summer wobbling about on the lake in an ancient canoe anxiously counting heads. While all this was going on, Maria was busy sorting out the infirmary supplies and I was helping prepare the day camp centre which involved such tasks as sawing the legs off tables so they matched all the little chairs that had been delivered. This wasn't as easy as you might think—in our efforts to make all the legs level and eliminate any wobbles, the tables themselves began getting precariously low. We were on the point of having to add limbo dancing to the curriculum when some potential rocket scientist saved the day by shoving bits of cardboard under the remains of the rickety legs.

The centre itself was the newest building at the camp and was still being finished off when we arrived. Besides the tables and chairs there were mattresses on the floor so the younger kids could take a nap, there were games, books, puzzles, paints and such like, plus a radio and tape player. Because it was so new, warm and clean compared to the rest of the camp, I found myself using the place as a little haven of peace and respite where I would sometimes escape in the evenings, turn on the radio and listen to French songs wafting in from stations across the Canadian border. As I was later to discover, the building also acted as a discreet love nest for two of the overseas counsellors whose mutual passion proved an effective antidote to the humdrum camp routine.

I might never have known what was going on had I not opened the centre one morning to find Monika's fashionable Italian suede jacket and very skimpy black bra still dangling from one of the miniature chairs. I grabbed the clothes and dumped them in our dressing-up box just as one of the regular earlybird mothers dropped off her little girl. Of course the child made straight for the box and promptly dragged them out again before marching towards us with the bra around her head, the cups sticking out like Mickey Mouse ears. Mum raised a brief, quizzical eyebrow but luckily was late for work and hurried off, the incongruous image of her eight-year-old padding around in slinky lingerie fading as she negotiated the narrow gateway out on to the road while simultaneously taking her umpteenth mobile phone call of the morning.

We had intended to spend the whole season, around nine or 10 weeks, at this camp, but for a variety of reasons we bailed out after just one month. The kids, though constantly demanding and draining, were fine and the rest of the counsellors were great, but the camp itself was pretty awful. Equipment and facilities, obviously the product of a shoe-string budget, quickly became very ragged, meals were marginally less appetising than refried road kill while our living space was so spartan we began to dream longingly about Trappist monasteries.

Maria and I shared a pre-fab cabin sandwiched between the sick bay and one of the kids dormitories. It was dirty, draughty and damp, and the ceiling constantly rained down bits of disintegrating gib board. Each night before putting out the light we would embark on a compulsory mossie extermination programme so within just a few days the walls began to resemble some garish piece of splatter art by Jackson Pollock. There was nowhere to hang anything and our clothes, which seemed permanently damp, were always spilling out of our cases and onto the sandy, muddy floor. It says a lot about the staying power of the other counsellors—who, after spending all day with the kids then had to sleep in dormitories with them—that they actually envied our accommodation. Hot showers were both a luxury and a lottery with just two shared between about 20 resident staff, while within a week of the camp opening it became horribly clear the toilets were chronically unable to cope.

The rest of the counsellors, snared to a great extent by the conditions of contracts they signed before leaving home, had little option but to grin and bear it. Stoically they resigned themselves to seeing out the summer season before heading off to explore as much of America as time and budgets allowed before returning to their respective countries, universities or jobs. Normally we would have done the same as the physical conditions alone were not so bad that we couldn't have endured for another month. But what made things much worse for us was that Judy, badly out of her depth trying to run the place, began to load us up with more and more jobs. She had one very capable assistant but as the only other two mature staff at the camp, we found ourselves increasingly relied upon for general administration, setting camp policy, planning activities and overall supervision of other staff. These burgeoning responsibilities were starting to loom over everything like a black cloud and seriously jeopardise our precious free time.

A single day off per week seems to be the general rule for summer camp staff and it was a measure of the gruelling, grinding routine that time off, especially away from the camp, was something everyone came to prize more highly than the meagre pay. Transport in this isolated Vermont camp was at a premium and it was never easy to get away from the place, particularly when the break was only for a few hours. The final straw came when we had to fight a move to make us take our days off separately so one of us remained always on duty. This was all getting so far from what we had been led to expect before we left New Zealand that we reluctantly decided to quit even though we knew it would make things tougher in many ways for those left behind. When we finally told everyone we were going a few people rather touchingly cried, though whether because we were leaving or because they were staying we were not sure.

The popular format for days off among overseas counsellors was to head for the nearest good-sized town and book into a motel for 24 hours. I'm sure many of the counsellors spent their time unwinding with a few too many beers, maybe a joint or two, almost constant television and loud music and, if they were lucky, getting laid. In our case, the pleasures were simpler. We'd start by standing under a hot shower for about 30 minutes, revelling in the privacy and secure in the knowledge that the motel had unlimited hot water and there was no jostling queue building up outside the door. Next on the list would be the hunt for real food.

Everything tasted better off camp but even so American food took a bit of getting used to. It was the unlikely combinations as much as anything. One of our first brunches featured waffles, strawberries and sausages, while it was always a little bit surreal watching people crumble scones and biscuits into their gravy at breakfast time. These brief forays into civilisation always meant stocking up with plenty of fresh fruit and vegetables; on the camp menu, even such humble fare as apples and oranges acted like reclusive celebrities and made only the rarest of public appearances. I hasten to add that sex also figured on our list of pleasures—right up there with fresh produce and toilets which didn't overflow. However, after sampling the sensual delights of an edible dinner, a bottle of wine, a midnight movie on TV, fresh sheets and a soft, warm bed, I cannot recall if we ever stayed awake long enough for anything else!

One thing which did impress us in Vermont, and indeed throughout the other parts New England we saw, was the patriotism of the local people, illustrated most clearly by their pride in the flag. The stars and stripes snapped from flagpoles on houses and in gardens throughout towns and villages, and decorated many an isolated farmhouse. At the summer camp there was a flag raising ceremony each morning, which everyone had to attend, and a lowering ceremony in the afternoons. Kids and counsellors stood with hands on hearts and even the most obstructive and difficult campers, when it was their turn, stood up and delivered a carefully prepared thought for the day.

There was also a well-intentioned effort to include a weekly campfire night aimed at teaching the kids something about Native American Indians. This involved the same few counsellors each time dressing up as Indians and arriving at the lakeside campfire in canoes. The idea was that they would then share stories and songs with the campers and talk a bit about Indian history and traditions. Unfortunately the first such Indian arrivals we attended were badly under-rehearsed and childish. Although the counsellors involved gave it their best shot they were always fighting a losing battle and the exercise did little more than provoke sniggers and silly jokes from the culturally insensitive and usually very tired campers.

We were in Vermont for the Fourth of July, Independence Day and the pinnacle of the nation's patriotism. In fact we enjoyed a double dose. July 3 happened to be our weekly day off so we hired a car and drove a couple of very scenic hours south to the state's largest city, Burlington. That night, despite persistent drizzle, a large crowd gathered down along the waterfront on the edge of Lake Champlain to watch and cheer a magnificent fireworks display. The following day we left just after 6am and sped back to our camp through villages already decked out with flags and bunting for their various Independence Day parades. Later that morning all the kids and counsellors from the camp joined the parade which noisily wound its way through our little local town. Every year the camp entered its own float and most of us marched alongside wearing garish paper caps in the camp colours and throwing sweets to children lining the route. For such a small community it was an amazing parade with lots of floats, loud marching music, bright uniforms, tons of food and drink, and a veritable forest of hand-held American flags as the whole town turned out for its annual birthday celebration.

Burlington had a great atmosphere with its bustling mall, Saturday street market stalls, buskers, cafes, lots of interesting shops and plenty of red corpuscles pumping through its heart via the University of Vermont campus. It was also the place where we thought our hire car and most of our possessions had been stolen and where we ended up tangling with the local sheriff's department.

We drove into town in our usual state of day-off euphoria, parked at the end of a row of cars and put our money in the meter. However, when we returned, no car! We assumed this was our first brush with the crime-ridden America we had heard so much about and dashed into a nearby cafe to call the police. However, we then received the good and bad news from the cafe proprietor—the car had not been stolen, but it had been towed away. It turned out we failed to see a tiny sign way up a pole saying our space at the end of the row of cars was in fact reserved for delivery vehicles. "Lots of folks git caught like that," the friendly cafe man tried to comfort us. "I seen dozens of 'em gitting towed." In many ways we were relieved as our luggage in the car included such hard-to-replace items as our CVs and references, plus things like address books and photo albums. However, we were also a bit pissed off being caught in such a sneaky way and now having to face some sort of sadistic treasure hunt all over Burlington to collect our $35 police ticket in one place and recover the car from the pound on the other side of town.

Luckily the cafe man turned out to be a born-again Christian with a sporty, convertible Trans-Am who very kindly agreed to chauffeur us around. First to the police department which seemed staffed entirely by seriously overweight officers. Bull necks, multi-storied chins and bulging stomachs festooned with hardware all remained completely underwhelmed by our puny protests about the injustice of it all and how something like this could ignite a diplomatic incident between Burlington and New Zealand. We'd have to put it all down in writing, they said, and send it to the city attorney's office.

We were seething by the time we got to the pound where we had to hand over $40 in cash there and then to get the car back. We vented our anger on a hapless, spotty youth shuffling around in oil-stained overalls. We demanded to know how they had physically towed the car and, as if playing an elaborate game of charades, made a great show of examining it minutely for any scratches or scrapes. We then jumped into the vehicle and would have swept imperiously out of the yard had not Maria clipped the bumper of a nearby parked car as she reversed. For a few graunching seconds the two cars were locked together like mating dogs and when they reluctantly parted we found ourselves completing a second, rather less haughty bodywork inspection.

Of course, the only damage was to our car and, avoiding eye contact with the now smirking youth, we drove away in a haze of venomous accusations about who was to blame for that little scrape. I would have though it was obvious—the driver. However, my wife came up with the novel defence that I should have been looking behind and warned her about the other car. "What were you doing, just sitting there?" she demanded to know, at the same time, it seemed to me, rather deftly defining the role of the passenger. Meanwhile, back at our lodgings we spent another testy hour using the hopelessly inadequate bodywork repair tools found under a motel sink to remove evidence of the collision from the grazed bumper and paintwork.

Next morning, re-united again in our determination to fight city hall, we called in to plead our case with the city attorney only to be told there was nobody we could see in person and we would have to put everything in writing. This we rather grumpily did in red biro on a crumpled piece of A4, reprising the indignant arguments which failed so miserably to bring the police sobbing to their knees—the sign was all but invisible, we were foreign visitors new to town, was this their idea of encouraging tourists, and so on. Later, when we returned the car to the hire firm, we parked it hard up against a wall, dropped in the keys with a cheery "Have a nice day" and hoofed off as fast as we could. We never heard anything from the car hire people but some months later in England we experienced a retrospective frisson of satisfaction when a reply from the Burlington attorney's office finally caught up with us saying they had decided to waive the $35 parking fine.

All our agonising over the decision to leave the camp was soon forgotten in the following few days of blissful freedom…no kids, real food, plumbing which worked and, above all, oodles of time and space to ourselves. At this stage we had no firm plans other than to head to Boston where we had made tentative job inquiries after seeing another summer camp advertising for a nurse. However, we decided to give ourselves a few days break first—if the job went in the meantime, then it was not meant to be and instead we would just do the touristy thing in Boston before leaving for England a few weeks earlier than intended.

So we took delivery of another hire car on our final evening at camp, threw in all our meagre belongings and drove to Canada. The fairytale feeling was enhanced by suddenly finding ourselves surrounded by people speaking French. That night we stopped only a few miles across the border in the little town of Sherbrooke where, in search of a B&B, Maria hastily resurrected her schoolgirl French. Within minutes we were the proud owners of two saddles, 10 yards of calico, a case of olive oil and shares in a holiday cottage on the outskirts of Ottawa. No, seriously, Maria was most impressive and with only the merest hint of mime we secured a double room and breakfast. The charming madame who ran the place either could not, or would not, speak a word of English, but next morning very kindly attached herself to us for an impromptu tour of the town.

Our next stop was Quebec where we had the good fortune to catch the end of the magical Summer Festival. On a balmy July night the narrow, cobbled streets of the old city were bursting with visitors; eating, drinking, laughing and singing, they tumbled out of restaurants, cafes and bars, and swarmed beneath the city's dominant landmark, Chateau Frontenac. Street entertainers were everywhere, class acts from many countries who travel a well-worn circuit around the world taking part in such stunning events. If the old city enchanted by night, it was equally appealing the next day when we opted for an official tour which turned out to be for just us and one other couple. Our guide was so good we insisted on taking him to lunch afterwards. We went to the Silly Pig, a fun little restaurant whose name sounded quite different in French, where he kindly and in great detail answered an endless flow of questions about the past, present and future of Canada, Quebec province and Quebec city. He was a mine of information as you might expect from someone who took tours to help subsidise his first love—working as a freelance television producer with his own current affairs programme.

We were smitten with the history and sheer beauty of Quebec and spent the rest of the day and night rambling around the old city. In fact it really quite spoiled us with the result that next day we were much less impressed with Montreal than we probably should have been judging by everyone's rave reviews. We saw the city from above—looking down on glistening skyscrapers from Mont Royal, the 790-foot parklike summit of an ancient volcano—and underground, on the famous whispering rubber-wheeled metro trains. Montreal obviously has a lot to offer but it couldn't begin to elbow Quebec out of our affections.

2

We returned the car to Burlington and decided to pick up another for the trip to Boston, an option which worked out fractionally cheaper and a great deal more convenient than buying two one-way bus tickets. We found car rentals in the States amazingly cheap and hassle-free though we never quite got used to the jaw-dropping size and sophistication of the juggernauts that go under the misnomer of "compacts". When they ask in advance what sized car we want we patiently explain there are just two of us and not much luggage so something small, economical and at the cheap end of the rental scale will do nicely. What you drive away in, on the other hand, closely resembles an air-conditioned, cruise-controlled bowling alley with reclining this and electronic that. True, it's probably not very good on petrol, but of course Americans compensate for this by practically giving the stuff away.

Visiting Bali later in the year we experienced a contrasting style of car hire. Some friends had given us the business card of a rental company where they had got a good deal about 18 months previously. By some fluke we found this place tucked away in a side street and launched into our spiel about how they came highly recommended and how well they had looked after our friends (nudge, nudge). However, it soon became clear the smiling scrum across the counter spoke little English beyond "You want Jimmy Jeep" followed by a quote which sounded like a wheelbarrow full of Indonesian rupiah. We had to ask them to write down the figure and then realised that whatever we said they would take the paper back and scribble a lower figure. Normal questions about insurance, fuel, maps, routes and return times all shaded the price down and final agreement was only reached when we ran out of things to ask.

We also found out that Indonesians, unlike Americans, don't believe in unnecessary paperwork...we set off in our Jimmy to explore the north of the island armed with little more than our credit card receipt. After a few miles two things quickly became apparent—police and other emergency service vehicles were conspicuous by their absence, and the local people, especially those on noisy little motorbikes, were suicidally reckless drivers. Bearing all this in mind, we drove extremely cautiously for the next few days, especially at those sign-less junctions where about eight roads meet, and made it back safely though not entirely accident-free. One day, while the Jeep was parked at the side of the road, a motorcyclist ran smack into it. We dashed out of a nearby artist's studio, our hands still full of beautiful batik prints, to find the rider was thankfully okay and so was our Jeep. With the help of several onlookers we managed to straighten out the motorbike, the rider jumped back on and disappeared at speed into the heavy traffic, a little bloodied but still beaming.

Somewhere between those extremes of East and West was Ireland. We were staying in a Dublin youth hostel and planned a few days touring over to the west coast and around the Ring of Kerry. We stopped at a panelbeaters workshop and asked an old boy where we could hire a car. He stood there rubbing his hands on a piece of oily rag, a look of blank confusion settling on his face as if he were trying to recall some complicated piece of quantum physics. "Aah now," he said at last, "I'll have to think about that one." As we only had a week in Ireland we carried on and headed for the nearest phone box. Thumbing through the Yellow Pages we suddenly noticed a card stuck up above the phone advertising Paddy's Auto Hire or something similar. The rates quoted were about half anything else we'd seen, so we gave Paddy a call. Oh sure he had just the car for us and wouldn't he bring it along in a few minutes if we'd care to wait inside the hostel.

Not long after, an impish little man arrived in reception, sat himself down with all the relevant papers for us to sign and then handed over the keys to the car which was right outside. Almost as a parting question we asked if it took unleaded fuel as most modern cars do now. "Well," he said after a short pause. "I find meself it runs a bit sweeter on the leaded." Suddenly alarm bells were going off in all directions...just how ancient was this car? When we got downstairs it was almost a relief to find it was only about 10 years old. However, it had certainly been well used and we all knew, though nothing was said, there was no point in the usual pre-hire inspection for scratches and dents. Lots of things inside no longer worked either, most unnervingly the front seat adjustment mechanism which meant whoever was driving was liable to shoot suddenly backwards or forwards without warning.

Most incongruous of all was a huge chain, the sort used to tether grazing elephants, bolted to the floor of the car under the driver's seat. It was a security measure, explained Paddy in a tone which suggested they were pretty much standard issue in cars these days. Whenever we parked we had to wrestle this chain through the steering wheel and fasten it with an equally elephantine padlock. By now we were growing a little anxious about what to do in the event of a breakdown, our concerns heightened by the discovery of a railway timetable in the dashboard. Again the same gentle Irish lilt: "Don't you go worrying about that now. If anything should happen just take it to the nearest garage...but be sure to have someone ring me first." However, Paddy assured us we'd no need to be thinking of such things, and remarkably he was right. Like a sturdy, well-trained pony, the car plodded reliably around Ireland and back to Dublin a week later, a little older and dirtier but with the elephant chain intact.

From Burlington we set off through Vermont, cut across a corner of New Hampshire and into Massachusetts, heading for Boston where we booked into the YHA for a week. Our only stop along the way was at Enfield, New Hampshire, to visit the Shaker village and museum. Visitors to this serene complex can't help but admire the plain furniture, innovative farming techniques and quiet simplicity left behind by this vanishing religious sect. Disappearing fast, of course, because members must remain celibate…"*No Sex Please, We're Shakers*". Indeed, men and women were once so strictly segregated that even during their rare dances they would not be allowed in the same room at the same time. For many years a steady supply of orphans maintained membership which peaked in the 1840s at around 5,000. But today recruits are few and far between and Shakers, once derided as "Shaking Quakers" because of their ecstasy during worship, are an endangered species.

Boston is a wonderful summer city though by all accounts a pretty brutal place in winter. We started on the third floor of the hostel but by the second night were promoted another seven levels to a large room with sweeping views up and down the Charles River. Directly across the river lay Cambridge, where we toured the hallowed turf of Harvard and its slightly less prestigious neighbour MIT, the Massachusetts Institute of Technology. We worked our way steadily through the guide book, ticking off the likes of Faneuil Hall, Quincy Market, the Hancock Tower and many other highlights, but the best things in Boston weren't always planned. We enjoyed jazz in a park by the river, chanced upon a stunning performance of *A Midsummer Night's Dream* in Copley Square, and spent a warm Sunday afternoon exploring Little Italy in search of an advertised parade marking the feast of St Rocco. We never found the parade but saw so much else.

At Wally's Bar we sampled blues and jazz though it was so loud that, even pressing ourselves against the furthest wall from the stage, we had to leave after an hour. The next night we opted for something quieter but much more exciting, joining 33,000 baseball fans at Fenway Park to watch the Red Sox snap a losing streak by thumping Kansas City. One of the intriguing things about baseball is the way spectators are allowed to keep the ball when it goes into the crowd. During this game they must have got through about 50 balls, a display of rather more conspicuous consumption than in English cricket where the ball is always politely tossed back to the players.

We had brought a calendar with us when we left New Zealand and had inked bright blue crosses on it to mark the passing of every week.

It became a fun ritual each Tuesday and we'd take turns to do the crossing off, usually with some small celebration for each little milestone—one week, a fortnight, a month, two months, wow! During those first few weeks and months we marvelled at how long we'd been away, at the places we'd visited and all the things we had seen and done. We still thought about home a lot, most often with the sheer delight of not being back there. Quite often, especially if enjoying a special meal, a great view or a trip to some new and exciting place, we would stop and deliberately try to imagine what our former work colleagues would be doing at that precise moment. Next came the same silly, almost rhetorical question: "Would you rather be here or back there?" It was an exercise which never failed to send our spirits soaring even higher! Of course, there were lots of things, or at least people, we missed, though the main one was our darling dog. Maria would sometimes have a little cry when she thought about Buffy…daft, really, but I think the pair of us shed more tears for him than we ever did for the kids!

By the time we reached Boston we had been away from New Zealand for seven weeks, which meant it was a full two months since I'd sat down at my desk to do any writing. I always intended to do some stories during our travels and had already spotted a couple of potential features in Boston which I was sure would interest readers back in New Zealand. Perhaps to help ease me gently back into work mode we took a tour of the mighty *Boston Globe* newspaper headquarters on the outskirts of the city. It turned out to be a bizarre experience as the rest of the tour party comprised a mentally challenged group from a local institution. We were gathered together by a bright young thing who warbled through an introductory talk about the paper's history, size, circulation, number of staff and so on. Before moving on to see parts of the production process in action, she asked if there were any questions. Without missing a beat a gravelly monotone from the depths of the group piped up: "Can we go home now?" The young woman smiled sweetly but didn't invite any more questions during the tour. I enjoyed the chance to look around such a large, well-respected newspaper though its credibility was slightly dented afterwards by some glaring errors in the handouts they gave us.

Tourism was a subject I had written a lot about over the years and the two stories which jumped out at me in Boston were both in that field—one about the famous *Cheers* bar, and the other about Duck Tours, a relatively new venture in the city. It immediately struck me how easy it was in the States just to walk into somewhere, say you're a journalist wanting to write a story, then sit back while they run around in circles trying to please you. Nobody asked for any identification or proof of who I said I was. Instead they just rolled out the red carpet, gave me their time, assistance and access to top people, and showered me with free this and complimentary that. In fact they were so trusting I could imagine some unscrupulous con artist turning this into a career, travelling around America (perhaps even the world?) living on his wits and ill-gotten freebies.

It's really the Bull and Finch but to countless tourists and many millions of television viewers it's *Cheers*, the bar where everybody knows your name. Characters in the long-running TV series of the same name, people like Sam, Diane, Rebecca, Frasier, Woody, Cliff, Norm and Karla, have become firm favourites with comedy fans worldwide. Which is great news for Boston whose only real connection with the show is that the outside of the Bull and Finch features on the opening credits: almost everything else is shot at Paramount Studios in Hollywood. But this tenuous connection has been enough to persuade the savvy owner to convert the interior to match the *Cheers* bar we see on TV and install a gift shop and themed restaurant upstairs. The result is so popular that people are queuing down the street most days before the doors open, after which they can't wait to take photos and get rid of their money. When I called in to look around and do interviews for my story I was treated to lunch in the restaurant and virtually offered my pick of *Cheers* memorabilia including a classy hardback book recounting the history of the bar and show. I enjoyed the lunch but refused the book and other gifts, not for any deep-seated ethical reasons but purely on the practical grounds that we didn't need the extra weight to lug around the world.

The Duck Tours use World War 2 amphibious vehicles to take passengers sightseeing around the streets of Boston before plopping into the Charles River and continuing the journey by water. It's a clever idea, now catching on in lots of other places, including London, and has proved a great way of recycling 50-year-old military hardware. When I said I wanted to write a story for publication in New Zealand, the company was as pleased and helpful as if I'd offered them page one of the *New York Times*. I did my interviews and collected background material before Maria and I were taken on a free tour and then given T-shirts and other Duck souvenirs. I didn't have time to write either of these features until we were in Australia several months later. By then I had the material for three others and in due course they appeared in several New Zealand papers. However, it was never the paying proposition I had hoped. When I worked it out as an hourly rate, I realised I would have been much better off flipping giant "eNORMous Burgers" (corny, I know, but that's really what they're called) in the *Cheers* restaurant.

By this time, after a solid two weeks of playing tourists, we found ourselves back in employment. Maria had landed the nursing job we'd seen advertised which turned out to be at a superb YMCA camp near the picturesque and historic town of Sandwich, on Cape Cod. In fact this was really two sister camps separated by a lake they shared for water activities—Burgess, the boys' camp on one side, the girls in Camp Hayward on the other. Kids normally came for two-week blocks and on the final night there were campfires on each side of the lake. We were based at the boys camp and at the end of their fires, after all the songs, jokes, guitar playing and games, came what we called the Camp Howl. The kids would first rehearse some little message with the counsellors and then, on a given signal, 150 voices would bellow it in unison into the night. The effect was electrifying. One, two, three…"We love you Hayward!", the message racing through the darkness, ricocheting off surrounding hills and finally skimming across the lake to the girls around their camp fire on the other side. A few moments listening to the sounds ebb away, then another minute of silence watching sparks dance from our fire. Then, from out of the night, more of a high-pitched shriek than a howl…"We know!"

Many camps had trouble attracting registered nurses who could easily spend their summers earning far more money almost anywhere else. As a result they were desperate to get their hands on an experienced and highly qualified RN like Maria and luckily I was slotted in almost as part of the deal. For a while it wasn't clear what I would be doing or even if I would have work but in the end I landed right in the butter with what I considered the plum de la plum job on camp—van driver. At least I always thought I was the van driver until camp finished five weeks later and I sought a reference from Gareth Thomas, a sparky little Welshman who was the director of Camp Burgess. When I read this I realised all along I had in fact been "Director of Transportation". Well, if I'd known that earlier, I'd have asked for a more money. As it was Maria was paid $250 per week and I got $150 which gave us a weekly income of $400 with all our food and accommodation paid for. By summer camp standards we were seriously rich.

But it wasn't just the money: in every respect this camp was infinitely better than what we had left behind in Vermont. With around 300 kids and some 60 staff it was more than three times the size; it was obviously better funded, physically far more established and better equipped; and it was run by a very dedicated, enthusiastic and professional crew, right from the directors on down through the group leaders and activity supervisors to the foot-soldier counsellors on the ground. The camp was set in fantastic surroundings, its cabins and other buildings sprinkled through pine woods above the lake. Our accommodation, despite again being attached to the health centre, was positively regal after Vermont, while the food was five-star fare compared to what we had been enduring—a salad bar at every meal, fresh fruit spilling out of bowls, separate vegetarian meals, plenty of warm chocolate chip cookies! In short, this was how we always imagined summer camp to be.

Van driving during the month or so before we arrived had been shared out among counsellors which proved a totally unsatisfactory system: nobody really wanted to drive in addition to their other duties which meant regular runs and timetables had become hopelessly haphazard. As in Vermont, free time here was highly prized and for almost all the staff the van was the vital link between work and play. My arrival was greeted with widespread relief and approval as it meant normal service was resumed. The counsellors' delight in having a regular driver was exceeded only by my own delight in being there.

We were ourselves picked up by the van in Boston. A young woman called Jessica was at the wheel taking two Spanish girls to Logan International airport to catch flights back to Spain. That was another thing we liked about this camp—it drew young campers from Europe as well as all across the United States. On our way back to the camp, about 65 miles from Logan, I cast secret admiring glances around this large, virtually brand-new van. It handled very smoothly and I could hardly wait to take her out for a spin, pump up the air conditioning, flick on the cruise control, and settle back in the comfy driver's seat with a large coffee in the drink holder and the radio playin' some good ol' country music. In fact, I hardly saw that particular van again as it was used almost exclusively for taking kids and counsellors on special week-long, off-camp excursions. Instead, I got to drive Big Bertha. I wonder if there has ever been any large plane, train, truck, boat or other vehicle which has not sooner or later been nicknamed Big Bertha. Okay, so the name wasn't original but it was somehow apt for the huge, ancient, dirty, sluggish, dented junk heap on wheels that masqueraded as the camp van. This monster could seat 14; sometimes we squeezed in a few more but usually it was at least half empty which only served to emphasise what a barren old hulk it was.

My working day stretched from about 10 in the morning until just after one o'clock the next morning, so I was always pretty late getting to bed. However, these 15-hour shifts were not really so bad; the hours just defined the edges of my daily timetable and in between trips I had plenty of opportunity to relax. Every day I made three trips each way to drop off and pick up counsellors in the trendy town of Hyannis, a holiday resort made fashionable through its long connection with the Kennedys. Hyannis was a straight half-hour run from the camp with the first ride in at 10.30am and the last one back at half past midnight. Anyone failing to make the pick-up point for the final run home either had to stay in town another night or fork out for a cab. Both options were expensive which provided enough incentive for most of my passengers to be ready and waiting on time. Five nights a week we also did a laundry run to Sandwich. Only a handful of counsellors went each time, the male ones usually lugging almost every stitch they owned in great kitbags of dirty washing which necessitated driving with the windows open, at least on the way there. These trips meant hanging around for a couple of hours until everyone was finished. Nobody minded. The counsellors smoked, read magazines, ate junk food from nearby shops, flirted with each other and fed fistfuls of quarters into washing machines, dryers and soap dispensers.

Another regular but less frequent route was the one we did that first day with Jessica to Boston airport. Ah, the dear old Logan run…an all-singing, all-dancing nightmare a) if we hit the rush hour, b) if we miss a turning, c) just trying to manoeuvre Big Bertha through traffic-choked freeways and access roads, and d) even at the airport where there was precious little information to help you choose between about half a dozen almost identical terminals. On my first run to Logan I had 10 Spanish kids, their chaperone and a mountain of luggage and would never have made it if I hadn't also managed to squeeze Maria in as navigator. Even then, in thick traffic and with no signs at those crucial times when you're desperate for them, we needed a fair slice of luck to avoid a wrong turn and having to go on to somewhere like Miami before we could turn around.

Finally, I found myself kept fairly busy with the doctor runs, carting kids, and occasionally counsellors, to a medical centre about 10 miles away. These trips were mostly generated by Maria and the other two camp nurses. This being litigious America, the general rule was to err heavily on the side of caution, or as they say stateside CYA—Cover Your Ass. As a result, all sorts of minor ailments and complaints were packed off to the doctor…just in case. The majority were seldom anything more serious than poison ivy (yes, Allan Sherman was right, kids really do get that at summer camp), little boys feeling homesick or plump girls with non-specific tummy pains. Sometimes I would have as many as half a dozen hobbling, groaning, pallid or blotchy campers in the van which I didn't mind at all as it guaranteed me plenty of time to catch up on all the magazines and newspapers in the waiting room.

Van driving was just about the perfect job, involving as it did minimum supervision and maximum freedom. I was able to get away from the camp several times a day and indulge in such luxuries as a little shopping or maybe stopping somewhere for a doughnut and coffee. Occasionally there were a few hassles—traffic jams, people double-booking the van or not turning up when they should—but these were minor irritations. Generally "work" was very pleasant, coasting through the leafy lanes and pretty little villages of Cape Cod on sunlit mornings, listening to good music on the radio, and on my midnight runs tuning in to the BBC world news. Driving here was also a pleasure because other road users were so incredibly courteous and polite. They would never hesitate to let you pull out in front of them while as a pedestrian the good manners of local drivers often bordered on the embarrassing. Standing casually just chatting at the curb you would glance up to see cars slowing almost to a standstill a good 50 yards away. With a cheery smile the drivers would gallantly wave you across the road and, so as not to hurt their feelings, you would cross whether you intended to or not, only to slink back again once they were out of sight.

I was constantly reminded of my good fortune whenever I saw the glowing faces of counsellors coming and going from their days off. Although these counsellors had an infinitely better deal than their counterparts in Vermont, they were still locked into long, intense days with kids, some of them also sharing cabins with the youngsters at night. Counsellors had to organise and supervise games, sports, social activities, even mealtimes, filling almost every hour of every day for campers who were often less than enthusiastic, cooperative or grateful. No wonder those guys were so happy when they jumped into the van to savour their thin slices of freedom. Even poor Maria didn't enjoy nearly the same relaxed routine as me. When not seeing kids during the daily clinics or handing out pills at mealtimes, she still had to be on camp in case some accident happened or to cover for a colleague's day off.

Sometimes when she managed to engineer a few hours break the first thing she wanted was to skip camp and perhaps just drive around local villages or into Hyannis. Recalling the dark days in Vermont I could easily understand how she felt even though, after all my driving and rushing about, I might have been happier just to flop in bed reading. Mind you, if I had done that I would have missed one of our most memorable evenings ever—open mike night at the Prodigal Son cafe in Hyannis. Among the musicians and poets who took the floor that night was a tanned and perfectly coiffured couple, probably in their mid-50s, from California. With the help of some pre-recorded very New Age sounds—tinkling crystals, bird song, whales, wind in the trees—these two began their act innocently enough with ancient Indian chants. But without warning they then launched into a part-spoken, part heavy breathing routine which appeared to end in simultaneous orgasms. Still fresh off the boat, we were absolutely gobsmacked. However, the locals, presumably accustomed to behavioural excess living just down the road from the Kennedy compound, seemed unimpressed. As the performers, flushed but still flashing perfect smiles, gathered up their bits and pieces, there was a faint smattering of applause before chat and cappuccinos washed through the cafe and carried them off stage.

Three registered nurses covered the girls and boys camps and just to make things confusing their names were Marie, Maria and Maree. Marie Hennessey, a Julie Andrews look-alike, was in overall charge. She was a lovely woman who was spending the summer at camp with her son, daughter and dog Kyla having left her husband behind chained to his desk somewhere near their home in Canada. Summer camp was Maria's first experience of the American health system and she was immediately struck by the amount of medication the kids brought with them. More often than not, after looking at the kids and checking their notes, she simply took the medicines away, telling them they could come and get something whenever they felt they needed it. Usually that was the last she saw of them until she handed the medicines back the day they went home.

These children were also remarkably well-informed about various ailments—their own and everyone else's—plus the pills and potions needed in each case. Because we were living in part of the health centre and I didn't have to get up until about 9am most days, I used to lie there listening to the kids on the steps outside as they queued up for the morning clinic. Most of them were regulars and the first worrying thing was that many would turn up 45 minutes early, as if this was the highlight of their day. Then they would stand outside, a bunch of eight to 13-year-olds going on 70, comparing symptoms, medications, prognoses and medical histories. It was if sickness was a status symbol and ill health something to be treasured and paraded like a badge of honour. "Looks like Mikey's got measles this week." "Measles! Huh, everyone's had measles. My sister's probably got scarlet fever and she says she's going to give it to me." "Well I've got this really neat rash on my lower back. My mom thinks it might be ringworm but the specialist she took me to isn't sure..." With fine dramatic effect he let the sentence trail off and for a few moments, amid a respectful silence from his peers, those last few words hung heavy in the air. Each savoured the implications of some mysterious medical condition so rare and no doubt so potentially dire that it baffled even a specialist. It was every American boy's dream…

At this camp we were again entitled to the regulation one day off per week and as there was so much to see and do on Cape Cod we decided to save up our days and take two together each fortnight. We used our first double banger to visit the Cape's two most famous islands, Nantucket and Martha's Vineyard, both very beautiful and steeped in history but perhaps best known as magnets for many of America's rich and famous. We first caught a ferry to Nantucket where residents have been able to use their power and influence to safeguard much of the island's original character and charm, keeping at bay many of the more tacky shops and businesses. The result is a rather quaint destination of twee houses, cute gardens and very expensive shops, the whole place oozing money while proudly proclaiming its links to a simpler age of seafarers and whalers.

That evening we had to trudge almost two miles through a hinterland of scrub and sand dunes to find the youth hostel where we encountered our first uni-sex dorm. The room was quite small and, by the time we arrived, quite full, so we had to resort to some judicious wriggling about under our single blankets to shed layers of clothes while trying to maintain a little modesty if not dignity. In Maria's case it was a wasted effort and she was mortified to wake up in the morning and find her blanket had slipped off during the night. "Oh well, worse things happen at sea," I said, rather cleverly I thought given the island's maritime history, but she was not amused.

Next day we wandered around Nantucket town and then joined an absorbing 90-minute bus tour of the island before boarding another boat to neighbouring Martha's Vineyard. We docked at Oak Bluffs around 6pm and, under the impression there were plenty of buses, we casually did some shopping and stopped in somewhere for supper.

Only then did we discover there were no more buses that day, we were six miles from the hostel and we couldn't afford a taxi. Now, we'd heard all the warnings about hitchhiking in America but, despite the approaching darkness, we couldn't really see much alternative. Maybe because this was Martha's Vineyard, home to laid-back rock stars and all sorts of other trendies, things were different here but within minutes we were riding along with a professional trombone player who worked everywhere from clubs to cruise liners. He took us part of the way and then the very next car along stopped and a couple from Chicago, both lawyers, went out of their way to drop us at the hostel door. Incidentally, this was the only place we've ever come across which maintains the old youth hostel tradition of everyone doing chores before they leave. These simple little tasks taking only a few minutes were written on scraps of paper and drawn out of a hat; our good deed was some sweeping and picking up those little bits of paper that people had just screwed up and dropped everywhere.

We shared a taxi back to Oak Bluffs which, with its colourful Victorian "gingerbread" cottages, has some interesting history but is nonetheless very commercial and tending towards seedy. Later we joined another excellent tour which visited the island's handful of other main towns, all of them, especially Edgartown, prettier and more appealing than Oak Bluffs. We caught an early boat back to the mainland as I was due to work again that night. We were supposed to be picked up by the van at 5.15pm but, despite several frantic phone calls, it didn't turn up until 6.30pm. By then I had begun to appreciate why everyone was so pleased when the camp employed a full-time driver…it was a hard job to combine with other duties. We raced back to camp where I had to collect an agitated group of counsellors who'd booked a late crossing to the Vineyard and then retrace the route we'd just taken. Plans for their precious day off were almost in tatters but, after driving perhaps a shade too recklessly, we just made it and they scrambled on board. However, being thrown around in the back of Big Bertha must have been more alarming than I realised. When I collected them next day they made a mock presentation of an unusual St Christopher, a small, red, fluffy Cape Cod lobster, called Chris. He did his job well, helping us all survive the summer unscathed, and is now enjoying retirement in my young nephew's toy box.

There were few rules attached to my job but one thing Bruce, the overall camp boss, insisted upon was that I never take people to the pub. The understandable logic behind this ruling was that if staff from the local YMCA summer camp were seen being dropped off at the boozer, it just might undermine parental confidence a wee bit. To avoid any such potential PR blunder, and given that staff were going to go to the pub anyway, an unwritten compromise was worked out. I could drop counsellors and other staff at a hole-in-the-wall money machine which just happened to be about 20 yards from the pub door. And so it was that expressions like "We're off to the bank tonight" and "See you later at the bank" entered the camp vernacular. Among the most regular customer for these nocturnal forays to the ATM was Liam, one of the Irish cooks. It was no coincidence that he also became one of Maria's most regular customers at morning clinic.

As we found in Vermont, counsellors and general staff made up a mini United Nations though at this camp Aussies and Irish were particularly well represented. The latter had been recruited virtually in one large group from the same area near Belfast and worked thankless long hours in the kitchens. Because they started very early in the morning, they also finished early and were entitled to skip camp several evenings a week. Their goal then, with lovable rogue Liam leading the way, would be to head for the pub and sink as many pints of Guinness as possible. It was no trouble to take people the 15-minute drive to the ATM but since there was never any set finishing time, the pick-up was more tricky. The normal arrangement was that if they were not standing outside I would just drive on past; occasionally, if I had time, I'd pop in just to see if anyone was ready to leave even though it meant risking the nightmarish sight and sound of Liam in mid Karaoke. His speciality was Frank Sinatra's *My Way* which he would tunelessly mutilate while sashaying around the rapidly-emptying bar. Once away from the monitor showing the words, Liam would simply begin to improvise while at the same time—completely oblivious to the thunderous looks from beefy boyfriends—trying to tempt every woman in the place to get up and dance with him.

Most nights the Irish contingent would stay until closing time, stumble back to camp and fall into bed for a few hours before having to face several hundred greasy fried eggs plus pagodas of pancakes with maple syrup. Not surprisingly by about 9 o'clock Liam would be feeling pretty fragile and would haul himself off to Maria complaining of a mystery virus. The short break from the heat and smells of the kitchen, together with the cold water and aspirins she prescribed, usually brought about a miracle cure and by the evening he was all set for another visit to the cash machine.

One morning Liam's bed was empty, he was nowhere around and worried friends covered for him on the early breakfast shift. Then about mid-morning I saw him getting out of a police patrol car at the end of the drive. He chatted with the officers sitting inside for a minute then shook hands and walked briskly up to camp. It transpired that he'd drunk several extra pints the previous night, fallen over outside the pub on his way to buy some cigarettes, been scooped up by the cops and taken back to the police station to sleep it off. In the end he'd had three more hours sleep than normal and someone had cooked him breakfast for a change, so he was feeling pretty chipper. Slipping on his apron to start preparing lunch, he maintained an air of studied nonchalance about spending time in an American jail. "Ah Jesus, sure I've been in lots worse cells than that".

It was a long two weeks between our days off but eventually it came round again and we were off exploring Cape Cod in a beaten up old Datsun borrowed from one of the American counsellors. However, dear old George, having got wind of my recent breakneck dash to the ferry for the benefit of some of his colleagues, only reluctantly agreed to let us borrow his car on condition Maria did all the driving. We spent nights at youth hostels in Eastham and Truro, but our main destination was Provincetown, nestling in the crooked finger at the northern tip of the Cape. P'town, as everybody calls the place, is renowned for two things—whale-watching and gay-watching. The whale-watching was superb and easily on a par with similar trips we've been lucky enough to make off New Zealand and Australia. In terms of value for money, it was probably the best—we paid just $29 for both of us and in glorious weather saw about 20 humpbacks, four minkes and a few dolphins, most of them quite close to the boat.

Back on dry land we wandered around the town, our naive little Kiwi eyes out on stalks. There was no disputing P'town's claim to be counted among the gay vacation capitals of the world. I've never seen so many men bulging beneath tight white T-shirts, short shorts and white socks. Others obviously felt more comfortable in leather miniskirts, sequined ball gowns or floaty chiffon, while pairs of butch women patrolled the streets with all the charm of rottweilers loose in a used car yard. I did my best to avoid eye contact with everyone. Maria was much more relaxed though I could have done without her running commentary…"Look! Look over there behind you. The one in the purple dress and pink high heels. He's gorgeous." Followed by a rather wistful and, I felt, quite uncalled for: "What a waste."

A week later summer camp was beginning to wind down, staff were saying emotional farewells to each other and everything suddenly slipped into cruise mode. For a few days I was busy ferrying people and their luggage to airports and bus stations but most of my regular daily runs were no longer needed. Maria and I found time to go out for a few meals, play tennis and even try rollerblading. This was very popular everywhere and it was wonderful to watch people gliding along at speed, stepping effortlessly on and off kerbs and ghosting through busy traffic. Of course, when you're the one strapped into the clumpy boots trying to move on those narrow sets of wheels, it suddenly becomes a whole lot more complicated and very much less graceful. We did manage to propel ourselves along a track by the canal for a couple of miles or so but in my case it was painfully slow going. Rigor mortis appeared to spread through my lower body and I had to keep coasting onto the grass and walking a few steps to re-establish contact with my legs. Most of the time Maria's better balance and greater determination meant she was not even in sight, and I admit I was a trifle miffed to find myself regularly overtaken by toddlers on trikes, arthritic dogs and little old ladies shuffling along with walking frames.

Things like eating out, going to the hairdressers and taking taxis exposed us to another unfamiliar but all-pervasive area of American life—tipping. I remembered this as a quaint English tradition from donkey's years ago when my mother, after taking us out for tea some-where, used to leave the waitress either threepence or sixpence under the saucer, depending on the service. In my mind that was always the key thing: the tip as an acknowledgment and reward for a job well done. But in modern America, tipping is an altogether different ani-mal—it's wild, unpredictable and bloody near compulsory. In fact many establishments have the cheek to include the tip on your bill and if you're not happy about that (and I'm usually not) you have to argue like hell with somebody to get it taken off again. Tipping in the States can quickly become a significant expense, especially if you're on a tight budget like we were, and it's also very confusing. People seem to tip anywhere between 10 and 20 percent, and in some places little ready-reckoners are available to help you work out the dollar amount.

The trouble now is people feel obliged to tip with the result that you risk massive guilt attacks—to say nothing of getting the grand stink eye from everyone in the place—if you don't ladle out great wads of cash to people just doing their jobs. My son, who has spent a fair bit of time waiting tables, naturally sees things differently and is always a generous tipper. He relies on the argument about the low wage structure in the service industries and how people like wait staff are dependent on their tips. In that case I reckon it's time to change the system. Take a leaf out of New Zealand's book by using well-trained, well-paid staff. Okay, the extra cost of that is built into your meal but I would rather pay a little more up front than have to endure terrible service and then be expected to reward wait staff for their rudeness, incompetence and indifference. While we were in America I was heartened to see this issue being lively debated in the media. Many people, it seems, are starting to challenge this robotic tipping which does little more than reinforce mediocrity and remove any incentive towards improving service.

While at the YMCA camp Maria had been studying to sit her American nursing exams which included getting used to imperial measurements again and learning lots of new drug names. The US system was such that the exam could only be taken on American soil and since we were here it seemed sensible to have a shot. We had vague plans of one day going to work in Colorado so, even though we were in Massachusetts, she arranged to sit the Colorado State Board exams. I dropped her at the testing centre in Boston on my way to the airport and for a few hours she sat closeted with a computer going through a series of multi-choice questions with no indication, even at the end, how she was doing. But a few weeks later, in England, we got the good news, little knowing then just how important that Colorado registration would turn out to be.

On September 1 it was time to leave Cape Cod on one last run to Logan airport only this time it was us catching a plane to Europe. As we drove over the Sagamore Bridge and off the Cape we found ourselves part of a ragged convoy of vehicles carrying unusually well-heeled refugees. Thousands of people were hurrying inland to escape the ravages of hurricane Eduardo which was spiralling its way along the east coast. A similar event a few years earlier had caused considerable damage at our summer camp but this time it turned out to be a false alarm and soon everyone was flooding back again. But not us. Our adventure was certainly continuing but on the other side of the Atlantic, in England.

3

The call came early one morning while we were in London. It was an emergency. That much was instantly clear from the tone of Gillie's voice on the other end of the line. Somewhere out there a little girl was in trouble. Could we help? How could we refuse? We were enthusiastic newcomers to the pet-minding and house-sitting world of Animal Aunts. We were dog lovers. Above all, we needed the extra money...

The customer in this case was Rinky Dink, a roly-poly terrier with bright button eyes which peered myopically through a curtain of dishevelled silky hair. Her owners both worked in the media and when mum was called away suddenly to Spain and dad had commitments at the editing studio, who else could they turn to but Animal Aunts? At first Rinky was hesitant about going off with two complete strangers and grounded her fat little bottom in mute protest. But with the help of a small dog biscuit she overcame her initial reluctance and, after a spell chasing pigeons and squirrels in the park, we were soon the best of buddies.

We looked after Rinky for two eventful days, the second etched for ever in our memories as Brown Thursday during which we learned much about the bowel capacity of small animals. For part of the day she was unable to "go" (though not for want of trying) and for the rest of the time she seemed unable to stop.

The trouble began when we got off a bus a couple of streets away from Leicester Square. As shoppers and commuters hurried by, a constipated Rinky began a strange crab-like dance along the pavement. However, it was not until we had settled down for an early lunch at a rather upmarket outdoor trattoria that her bowels finally moved, fortunately during the interval between the waitress taking our order and returning with the pasta. The result would have done a doberman proud and only some rather deft footwork enabled us to dispose of the evidence before its presence became painfully apparent to other diners.

Rinky really perked up a bit after this while her bowels positively went into overdrive. No sooner had we got home than the first stream of brown liquid became horribly obvious. We cleaned her up, gave her a bath and shampoo and dried her off. Delighted by all the attention she performed again. We repeated the cleaning and bathing regime, she pooped some more. Eventually she ran dry. We cleaned her up once more and, with every hair gleaming, gratefully delivered her home.

Rinky Dink was just one of a long list of comical and lovable characters we encountered over the next two months while working as Animal Aunts, a job we now look forward to each time we return to England. There are a number of similar agencies around the UK and no doubt others elsewhere in the world. But we like to think that Animal Aunts must be the most eccentric, wacky, jolly hockeysticks, frightfully British of them all.

We fell into this most wonderful of working holidays quite by chance. New Zealand friends had spent part of one summer as Aunts and casually left us the agency's card. This was months before we started our travels but once we knew we were heading to England we contacted the agency, sent off the required references and arranged an interview date. Interview is perhaps not quite the right word. When the door opened at Animal Aunts headquarters at Headley Down, in deepest Hampshire, we were engulfed in a tide of dogs of all shapes, sizes, ages and breeds. For the next couple of very informal hours we squeezed onto a sofa with most of this pack while Gillie McNicol told us about the agency and entertained us with stories from the Animal Aunts Archives. Strangely enough, though coming from the other side of the world, we found we were following a well-trodden path—at any one time there could be around 40 to 50 New Zealanders and Australians on the books. Perhaps it's because they tend to stay longer, maybe it's their practical streak, or possibly Gillie was simply buttering us up when she said Kiwis and Aussies tend to make excellent Aunts.

The eccentricity of the English, their love of animals and remnants of the British class system probably all play a part in the success of Animal Aunts. Gillie started the business in 1987. Returning to England after working with animals in Greece for six years she found herself in demand among friends as a house and animal sitter. Today she has built up a successful cottage industry with more than 5,000 regular clients being looked after by a constantly changing army of close to 400 Aunts working throughout Britain and occasionally further afield. Gillie runs the business from her hideaway home with the help of a computer-whiz husband and a handful of staff; even her mother is roped in to play her part, producing the company artwork which includes the cutest of Christmas cards each year.

The staff beaver away amid shrilling telephones, whirring computers and an ever-changing kaleidoscope of dogs in one smoky, totally chaotic office. They are a delightful crowd, all slightly off the wall in different ways which is no doubt how they probably regard many of the people working for them and even some of their clients. Once when we rang to find out about a job there was such a piercing shriek of anguish down the phone we thought a naked, knife-wielding maniac must have suddenly burst into the office. After an agonising pause the normal sweet voice resumed: "Sorry about that. Some jam from my doughnut just dripped on the computer keyboard."

Ringing the office to ask about jobs is a most exciting lottery. You just never know if you'll be offered a couple of labs in London, a pony in Peterborough or a kitten in Kidderminster; or for that matter a mouse in Manchester, a rat in Rochdale or a ferret in Folkstone. At the same time you discuss assignments and get details of the animals, you are quite likely to hear a much more interesting run-down on the owners and some of their idiosyncrasies. The beauty of it is you don't have to accept any job you don't want. If the animal, location or dates don't suit, you just say so and wait for something else to come along. Dogs, cats and horses are the most typical animals on offer, followed by chickens, ducks, sheep, cattle, pigs and goats. There are often fish—from minute tropicals in heated tanks to huge shadowy things which emerge from the depths of lakes to snatch whole loaves of bread before disappearing again—and all sorts of little furry things in cages. Sometimes, of course, the job can take on a distinctly exotic flavour when the family pet turns out to be a snake, llama, monkey…or parrot.

The first time I met Lorena she came strutting across the dining table towards me making alarming bobbing gestures which had me glancing anxiously around for a handy baseball bat. She was certainly beautiful but as we were to find out later, this brilliantly marked macaw was also highly unpredictable, destructive and wilful. On the first evening we were introduced, Lorena's proud owners explained that, with very few exceptions, she didn't like women and was generally pretty choosy about all her friends.

We were in a huge, expensively furnished apartment in the trendy north London suburb of St John's Wood where the annual rent alone was three times my old salary. Maria and I were sitting at the table talking to the couple who lived there—a charming American psychotherapist and her husband who's something big in the chemical business. Or is it oil? I'm finding it hard to concentrate. What's distracting me is this rapidly approaching painter's palette on claws with a beak capable of splitting open brazils or, more worryingly, any other nuts in its path. Our hosts, besotted parrot people, explain that the bobbing is a sure sign she likes me and they encourage me to extend the hand of friendship, literally. Reluctantly I do so and within minutes the bloody bird has crunched one of my shirt buttons to powder and nipped a neat hole in my best trousers.

Lorena enjoyed being stroked and tickled but I was warned by the owners to be careful where I touched her. Parrots, it seems, have a G-spot, and inadvertently sending the wrong message to a suddenly amorous macaw can be extremely hazardous to your health. The man of the house happily walked around with Lorena on his shoulder but as I rather liked my eyes and ears the way they were, I decided against that. Instead I carried her about on my hand and arm which was painful enough—whenever she wobbled, she dug in her claws for extra grip and invariably drew blood. She also liked to assert some kind of dominance by using my arm as a ladder to my shoulder, trying to scramble up so she was higher than me. I was almost always able to foil these attempts but once she made it and the only way I could get her off—Maria, revelling in my discomfort, was absolutely no help—was to lie on the floor and wait several minutes until she decided to clamber down onto the carpet.

Macaws, coming originally from tropical rain forests, also love bathtime and here our genial host used to oblige by taking Lorena into the shower with him. Like some sort of masochistic lunatic, he suggested I might want to try that. However, clinging to the hope that I still had many years of use for all my appendages, I politely declined and instead opted for Plan B, one of those trigger-action plant sprays filled with warm water.

The other bird we were looking after for the next 10 days was a much more friendly and likable sulphur-crested cockatoo called Wilfreida, or Wilfie for short, who used to climb down her perch and waddle along like Charlie Chaplin, following us from room to room. These two lived in the lap of luxury. They each had three elaborate and spacious cages—a night cage, a day cage and a travelling cage—and their toys arrived by mail order from the United States. We had to take the birds out of their cages several times a day for "loving", a period for playing with them like children and generally giving them the undivided attention they constantly craved. As far as Lorena was concerned, however, playing with her toys was always second choice behind inflicting some serious GBH on the fixtures and fittings in the apartment. With their wings clipped the birds could not fly but Lorena's favourite trick was to glide down onto a table or chair and instantly begin biting great chunks out of it; or she would grab a book or magazine and use her powerful beak to shred it in seconds.

In an optimistic effort to protect the furniture and expensive rugs, these birds had also been to some extent toilet trained. This party piece involved holding them at arms length over a piece of newspaper on the floor and uttering the word "kerploppo" with a heavy American twang. Lorena and I spent some time practising this manoeuvre though it was successful only twice. I was delighted each time though never quite sure if the bird was being clever or if I had literally scared the shit out of it with my ridiculous phony accent.

While the welfare of the pets is of prime importance, it's only part of the story. Animal Aunts provides a total package, beginning with the security of what are undoubtedly some of the most sumptuous and beautiful homes we have ever seen outside the covers of glossy magazines. This often means grappling with temperamental alarm systems and having to master codes, number sequences and other instructions which would have given the Enigma boys a run for their money. The usual scenario goes something like this…come back from walk tangled up in muddy dogs and dog leads, arms full of milk, post and morning papers, kick off wellington boots, fumble for keys, fall into kitchen, alarm starts beeping, stub toe on Aga, punch in code while hopping around in agony, alarm still beeping, muddy dogs disappear into immaculate lounge, hit "clear" and try code again, Christ it's still beeping, start panicking and expecting police and security people to come screaming up any minute, about to try code a third time when beeping stops, realise have missed phone call.

From posh London pads to ancient country houses, the homes of Britain's aristocratic animals need to be kept clean and tidy, and definitely left sparkling the day the client is due back. The same goes for the garden where jobs such as weeding, mowing grass or sweeping up leaves will be noticed and appreciated. Even in places that come complete with their own domestic staff (we rubbed shoulders with an army of cleaners and gardeners) there is plenty to do around grounds which

often seem to spread into two or three counties. Other nice touches
sure to please the client include a welcoming meal on returning home,
fresh flowers in the rooms and some basic shopping left in the cupboards. Of course, there are even more subtle ploys for those not above
a little brown-nosing...for example, a brightly coloured ribbon around
the pet's neck always leaves a lasting favourable impression.

In return for all this "work" Animal Aunts enjoy a tantalising whiff
of the good life. For a little while they are able to live in those beautiful
homes and very probably drive one of the client's flash cars. At different stays we were delighted to be handed the keys to Range Rovers,
Volvos, Land Rovers, BMWs, Saabs and several other vehicles all much
newer and grander than we could ever afford. We always nod sagely
with those who declare a car is only a means of getting from A to B.
But as you're playing with all the electronic gadgetry in the Beemer or
being pinned back in your seat by the acceleration of the turbo Saab,
you do come to appreciate there are another 24 letters in the alphabet.

We initially spent two months in England as Animal Aunts. During
this time none of our animals was more colourful, literally and figura-
tively, than the parrots but we were lucky enough to look after several
other real characters. One such job took us to a delightful picture postcard village in Surrey where the ages of most houses were counted in
centuries. The same could be said for a lot of the residents, but not
all...among the rich and famous associated with the district were Eric
Clapton, Harry Secombe, Richard Branson and Alfred Hitchcock.

Our sole charge here was a friendly wire haired dachshund who, like
so many of those stocky little canine characters, just had to be called
Buster. His passions were walking and ambitiously trying to hump
anything else on four legs. He loved going out so much that for the
first half mile he would scrabble furiously at the end of his lead, his
front paws barely touching the ground and practically garroting himself in the process. About the only thing he didn't like was being
groomed. At the first sign of his brush he would slink off with eyes
downcast and hide behind the couch until the "danger" had passed.

We always look forward to meeting the clients and spending some time with them—maybe only an hour or two but often as much as half a day or an evening which means we can share a meal and swap stories. This time is also vital for gathering all the information we are going to need while they are away. Once they've disappeared down the drive it's a bit late to be wondering where they keep the spare key, the fuse wire or the TV remote. So before they take off for Totnes, Toronto or Tobago, we need to know everything to do with their animals—from feeding, to walking, to vets—and their house—from watering pot plants, to forwarding post, to dealing with the man who's coming on Thursday to fumigate the wasps nest in the roof.

The agency sensibly provides clients with a very comprehensive check-list in advance covering all the important things. In addition, we have found many people, old hands at the game, have developed their own sets of very detailed instructions, often running to several typed pages. However, at a sit in Turner's Hill, just south of London, we were left in no doubt about how royally the two dogs were to be treated while the owners were away. The young grand-daughter in the house had written out a tongue-in-cheek menu for Maggie, an aging black labrador, and Shelley, a poodle: "Maggie and Shelley like a full cooked English breakfast in the morning, with English breakfast tea for Maggie and espresso for Shelley. Lunch—They like smoked salmon and caviar bagels with freshly squeezed orange juice. Dinner—Shelley has roast venison on a bed of sauteed red cabbage with pommes frites; Maggie will have chicken cordon bleu with a lightly dressed green salad and pommes frites. Both like a good red wine and a cigar!"

On another occasion I went off by myself just for 24 hours to look after four golden retrievers—an assignment I relished since I grew up in a house where we were constantly stepping over or around five gold-ies, plus regular litters of puppies. Even so, these four required a bit of Kissinger-like diplomacy at all times and I was left meticulous notes on each one. George was the boss and an underlined note in his file caught my eye: "He has only growled twice in six years but if he does it means trouble". If George spoke I was to pull any dog near him away quick using such authoritative voice commands as "Biscuits!", "Daddy's home!" or "Want to go for a walk?" Max was second in command and very highly strung "but he won't bite as he's all mouth and no trousers." Next came Denny, described as fat, laid back and lazy who liked to stay indoors or sleep on a sun lounger in the garden. After any meal, said my notes, Denny has "urges" directed at anyone nearby and not always well received by George or Max! Last but not least was sweet little Rupert, the baby of the family…and a thief. According to his file he had quite eclectic tastes and loved to steal food, jumpers, tin openers, rubber gloves and socks, and was especially fond of shoes.

The feeding regime was suitably complicated while the sleeping arrangements read a bit like that riddle about the fox, the goose and the corn. For example, Rupert could be put in with George or Max "but under no circumstances put George with Max or Denny as you may have world war three on your hands." If a fight did start the owners guaranteed it would be between George and Max, in which case I was to try the walkies and biscuit bribe words and if that didn't work they suggested the hosepipe, bowls of water…"or throw things!" Luckily these lovely dogs lived in a huge house and had the freedom of about an acre of well-fenced garden. Because I was there only one day the clients said not to worry about attempting a walk. Which was probably just as well as any outing doubtless required a separate book of instructions!

When arriving at a new sit it also helps to know what the house rules are regarding pets though our experience suggests most owners are just a bunch of great big softies. There may be some strict-sounding talk initially about who can go where and do what, but before long everything is being qualified and each rule has several exceptions. This was beautifully summed up in a list of Dog Rules published in one of the Animal Aunts occasional newsletters. I think it's a list most dog owners can readily identify with:

1. The dog is not allowed in the house.

2. OK, the dog is allowed in the house but only in certain rooms.

3. The dog is allowed in all rooms but has to stay off the furniture.

4. The dog can get on the old furniture only.

5. Fine, the dog is allowed on all furniture but is not allowed to sleep with the humans on the bed.

6. OK, the dog is allowed on the bed but only by invitation.

7. The dog can sleep on the bed whenever he wants but not under the covers.

8. The dog can sleep under the covers by invitation only.

9. The dog can sleep under the covers every night.

10. Humans must ask permission to sleep under the covers with the dog.

As Aunts we earned around 24 to 30 pounds a day depending on what, and how many, animals we looked after. The actual payment scale, if there is one, remains a mystery to us. Often we have found ourselves with the same combination of animals, say two dogs and a cat, for quite different fees. It might have something to do with how long the client has been on the books but we like to think it's just another of the agency's unfathomable foibles. Travel costs between jobs are met by the client and Aunts are paid a weekly allowance of 35 pounds towards fresh food while still allowed to gently plunder the client's cupboards, pantry or vegetable garden.

This unfettered access to other peoples' food stores has given rise to an unofficial but amusing "competition" which sometimes features in the newsletters…finding the oldest food. Aunts cheerfully but anonymously report unexpected encounters with tins and jars lurking in the

dingy recesses of cupboards or forgotten on dusty shelves with use-by
dates stretching back into the mists of time. Some contributors have
triumphantly unearthed relics still displaying pre-decimal prices which
dates them at least back to early 1971. We have not so far managed
anything close to those Methuselahs of the grocery world. But we can
claim several rusty, ominously bulging tins whose labels, well chewed
by generations of silverfish, identify them as some sort of oriental seafood. Then, of course, there are the countless pounds of home-made
preserves, standing in neglected regiments of jamjars, now well and
truly preserved beneath thick, fluffy blue duvets of mold.

Food though is one thing, booze quite another. We have often
found ourselves working for people who have more alcohol around
their houses than the average off-licence. Quite a few boast imposing
wine collections. Often they are extremely generous and with an airy
wave of the hand as they set off on holiday they tell us to just help ourselves to anything we want. However, drawing on some bitter experiences, the agency has fashioned sensible hands-off guidelines when it
comes to clients' booze. In the dim and distant past it was not
unknown for the help-yourself approach to result in some very contented Aunts happily sculling back bottles of Chateau Lafite '45 with
their fish and chips followed by After Eights, coffee and 19th century
brandy chasers. In the interests of maintaining harmony and avoiding
the necessity for the client to administer a sound horse whipping, the
agency recommends a different response. Instead of the words "help
yourself" triggering repeat trips to the recycling centre with barrow
loads of empties, the correct response suggested is to thank the client
and then ask them to put aside a bottle (or two) for you to enjoy during your stay.

Our first stint as Animal Aunts finished in fine style with a 17-day
stay at a seaside holiday cottage on the south coast near Bournemouth.
Here we took charge of Digby and Darcy, two Westies (west highland
white terriers), and a 40-something-year-old tortoise while the owners
were on holiday in China. The dogs were a couple of little dynamos,

tearing around at 100 miles per hour, always ready for a scrap with dogs five times their size and even attacking the television once when some lions appeared during a nature programme!

Minnie the tortoise was by far the easiest pet we have had to care for. She was not interested in eating or drinking and our only instructions were not to lose her in the garden and to prevent her starting to hibernate before the owners returned. She spent most of her time slowly ambling around the house like a meat pie on legs, laboriously navigating her way over any obstacles in her path, including prostrate terriers, and occasionally marking her progress with a bright yellow stain on the carpet.

A short piece of nylon cord, threaded through a small hole in her shell, could be attached to a rope in the garden, enabling her to roam about in the sunshine on warm days without fear she would make a sudden dash for freedom. Indoors she forlornly trailed the nylon cord behind her wherever she went, leading Maria to dub her with a rather unkind nickname. I often wondered what the neighbours must have thought when we came home and they heard Maria going through the house calling "Tampax! Tampax, where are you?"

Now, I have to admit there's a black side to Animal Aunts, and I'm talking here about the necessity for poop scooping. Once upon a time nobody batted an eyelid about where dogs did their business and in Paris, as visitors who have to wade ankle-deep through the stuff will know, they still don't. But in most parts of England now, owners who fail to clean up behind their dogs can face severe fines. One of the benefits of animal sits deep in the countryside, with easy access to woods and fields, is that you seldom have to worry about picking up, whereas in urban areas it's almost always plastic bags at 40 paces. When concern about the health and environmental implications of dog droppings began to grow, a few entrepreneurs saw the opportunity to make money by inventing elaborate pooper-scoopers. For a variety of reasons these never really caught on, mainly I suspect, because people are not terribly keen on stinking, dog-shit encrusted devices cluttering up their cars or garages. That, plus the fact plastic bags are cheaper (in some parks they are sensibly provided free) and do the job better.

Having said that I must confess picking up a warm squishy one left behind by a large dog—knowing there is only a micro-something of plastic between it and your fingers, and then having to cradle it like a packed lunch for maybe another mile or two on your walk—is not a pleasant experience. In fact I must go further and confess there have been occasions when, after a furtive look around to make sure no one is watching, I might have booted the offending pile out of sight or simply ignored it and hurried on. Some of the trickiest situations arise when your dog turns out to be a "hopper"; that is, he doesn't stop to do his business but carries on half walking, half hopping, leaving a trail of pieces behind him. These trails are particularly awkward, being equally difficult to ignore, hide or pick up.

One of the west highland whites was a hopper and in his case I adopted what Baldrick would no doubt describe as a cunning plan. There were some pine trees in a park we passed through with the dogs and the cones were almost exactly the size and shape of this dog's droppings. Like a magician setting up a simple trick, I slipped a few of these into a plastic bag and carried it with me. Whenever Digby (or was it Darcy?) started hopping I would bring out my pre-filled bag with a theatrical flourish, give a good-natured shrug and a cheery wave to any other dog walkers in sight, and briefly squat down. Then, holding my little bag of pine cones rather ostentatiously for all to see, I would walk on. Maria used to say I was being childish and, in view of the metaphorical mountains of pooh I have moved since, I suppose she was right. But at the time I think she secretly enjoyed the phantom poop scoops as much as I did.

We spent the whole of September and October in England which seemed very small and crowded after America. It was our first time back in the UK for nine years and that had been only on holiday; it was more than 17 years since we'd lived here. It didn't seem worthwhile buying a car just for two months and instead we spent a lot of time and money travelling on buses, trains and the London underground. We were surprised at how busy and congested England was. Even in country towns and villages traffic would often be brought to a standstill along streets and roads never designed to cope with such volumes of cars and lorries. Once safely installed at a new animal sit, we used to take perverse delight in listening to the early morning news and traffic reports. Bad weather here, an overturned lorry there, a train breakdown somewhere else; traffic backed up for miles on the M25, commuters facing lengthy delays on their way out of London tonight; drivers warned to avoid this area, roadworks causing hold-ups in that area. Oh, sheer bliss on a blustery Monday when you're still warm in bed, wondering whether to tackle a third slice of toast and another cuppa, still only halfway through *The Times*...

Later, when living in America, radio traffic reports from some of the large cities became required listening in the morning purely for their entertainment value. There seems no end to the weird things which clutter American freeways during the rush hour. The roads must resemble rather haphazard showrooms with a good selection of sofas, armchairs, tables, carpets and other miscellaneous home furnishings. Meanwhile the do-it-yourself enthusiast's drive to and from the office can be spent eyeing ladders and various trade tools, along with timber, plastic piping and sheet metal. There's plenty of clothing out there, a very reasonable selection of fruits and other foods, unlimited car parts, stray animals and much more. But perhaps the best we ever heard was the broadcaster advising drivers on a particularly busy Los Angeles freeway to watch out of a five-foot weather balloon!

Although we were looking after animals and houses pretty much the whole time, there were short gaps in between sits which gave us the chance to catch up with family and friends. We called in on various siblings and cousins dotted around England and were also able to see my mum and sister, then both living in Cape Town but visiting the UK on holiday. At one of our country sits we hired a small barn attached to the village pub and arranged a Sunday afternoon get-together for about 20 old friends and some of their children. We also indulged in a little more nostalgia by going back to the homes where we grew up—mine near Norwich and Maria's on the outskirts of Barnsley—and to the 250-year-old red brick terraced cottage in Wiltshire where our own kids spent their first few years. Stepping back into the past like that is always a bit weird, particularly the way in which places seem much smaller and distances much shorter than they used to. It was even more strange to find some of the neighbours were still there, living in their same houses, in one case more than 40 years later. Strange, I suppose, because in that time our lives had changed such a lot—we had moved to New Zealand for a start—while theirs, it seemed to us at least, had hardly changed at all.

In a post office in America we once saw a notice reminding "snow birds" about having their mail forwarded. When we asked someone to translate the message we found "snow birds" was the rather lyrical name given to those retired folk who flock each winter to the warmth of Florida or other southern states. By the end of October in England we began to feel a distinct chill in the air and, like migrating birds ourselves, we were ready to fly south before winter started to bite. When we took stock of our fairly threadbare finances it was a pleasant surprise to find we were leaving with almost exactly the same amount of money we had when we arrived. In other words, we had enjoyed two months in England, hired a car and spent plenty of time socialising, all paid for out of our Animal Aunts earnings. It had been, in effect, a free holiday, which is pretty much the way our subsequent house and pet-sitting has worked out too.

4

We flew out of Heathrow bound for Bali. At Singapore we connected with another flight which, a couple of hours later, touched down in the heat and humidity of a tropical night in Denpasar. Since we embarked on this gypsy lifestyle, living and working in different parts of the world, we have racked up some serious mileage. Our round-the-world tickets have been with either Qantas or Air New Zealand and we have amassed quite a few frequent flyer points with both these major carriers and their partner airlines. However, we have never been in the same league as those compulsive business travellers who practically live on planes and whose homes grow to resemble the inside of a 747 after a long haul with their accumulation of shapeless socks, mini tubes of toothpaste, washbags and eye masks. So, unlike such seasoned voyagers, we never seem to achieve the status required to breeze into those plush airport lounges usually glimpsed only through the frosted portholes of heavy mahogany doors.

Not that we haven't tried. Hardly an airport goes by where we don't stagger through a set of those doors, approach the smiling and immaculately groomed young man or woman at the desk and optimistically hand over our boarding cards with a brief supporting statement about the value of our patronage to this particular airline. They in turn, perfect smiles still intact, gently explain it's not possible, the subtext of their diplomatic refusal being that cheapskates like us can't stick our noses anywhere near this corporate trough and are Sir and Madam aware McDonald's, hard seats and peasants are on the next level down. But just once, on this trip through Singapore, we got lucky. We presented our shiny new Qantas frequent flyer membership cards at the desk and, with hardly a glance, were waved through to the inner sanctum. After something like 12 hours in the air it was wonderful to walk into a spacious bathroom area with soaps, lotions and potions, shaving gear, steaming hot showers and mountains of fluffy white towels. After pampering ourselves there we headed into an adjacent emporium of luxury to graze on trays of sandwiches, cakes and other snacks which could be washed down with a selection of drinks, alcoholic and otherwise, all absolutely free. Finally sated, we sank almost out of sight in a pair of cavernous armchairs and whiled away the rest of our stopover reading Australian newspapers. It's never happened again since, but we continue to live in hope.

It was hot, sticky and just after midnight when we arrived in Bali so we decided on the easy option and caught a cab to a much more expensive hotel than we would normally use. We reached the hotel the same time as a mini monsoon struck Denpasar and got absolutely drenched scuttling like crabs with bags over our heads between the taxi and our room. Indonesia was incredibly cheap after England so even the expensive hotel was only around 30 pounds; nevertheless, next day we took another taxi into Kuta and trudged the streets looking for something quite a bit cheaper. There were rooms available for about two pounds per night but they were just bare concrete boxes with bunks, most of them heaving with young male Aussies, their surfboards, sixpacks and sheilahs. So instead we settled on a compromise, a traditional-type Balinese hotel where bed and breakfast cost a very reasonable 12 pounds. I dread to think what kind of wildlife might have been lurking in those two-pound flophouses as even in the bath at our hotel we found a scorpion which gave an evil goodbye wave with its tail as Maria flushed it down the plug hole.

We spent a week on the island of Bali and a week on the neighbouring island of Lombok. Though both rely heavily on tourism, they could hardly be more different. Bali's main towns were thick with hawkers and stallholders selling everything from T-shirts to toys to barbecued sweetcorn, while budding Arthur Daleys stake out street corners ready to ambush passing tourists with cases of cheap watches and jewellery. These salesmen are all immensely persuasive and persistent but also incredibly friendly, seldom trespassing over the boundary into rudeness or aggression. Bali is one of those places where everyone expects you to haggle but that's not easy when the opening price already seems such a bargain. You don't have to look far to find evidence of poverty in Bali and every time we knocked a few rupiah off the price of something we were uncomfortably aware we were taking a little bit of money from the pockets of people who needed it far more than we did. After a while though, in the heat of haggle battle, you sometimes forget these scruples and the strength of your own currency and try to screw the price of a pineapple or batik print through the floor. When that happens you can't resist a small glow of satisfaction which lasts only until you pass a nearby shop window and notice scores of identical items all at half the "rock-bottom" price you just paid. No wonder those street traders are always smiling!

On just our second day we fell into a mini buying frenzy which saw us carting sandals, skirts and tops, dresses, shorts, shirts and sunglasses back to our hotel. Of course as soon as we emerged in all our sparkling new finery we became instant targets for every street vendor in Bali. We sought refuge on the beach but it was hopeless and we were soon surrounded by hoards of hawking harridans all tugging gently at us like a shoal of nibbling fish. In desperation I bought two pairs of batik shorts which even at the time didn't seem quite my size. Later, in the sanctuary of the hotel, I could hardly get the bloody things over my knees. Maria managed to squeeze into them but there was still something strange about the shape and then we realised what it was…in an effort to economise on material, they had all but eliminated the crotch. We eventually left them at the hotel in the hope staff there might know an 11-year-old crotchless anorexic midget whom the shorts would fit perfectly.

In our continuing efforts to blend in with the locals I had also bought a colourful shirt and matching wrap-around lavalava which I slipped on one evening as we were about to go out for a meal. However, the hotel proprietor stopped us as we passed the reception desk and diplomatically explained I had tied the garment wrongly, gathering it at one side the way local woman do instead of in front like the menfolk. It seemed a fairly fine distinction but who knows, in this unfamiliar and exotic location, perhaps an important one. She kindly called her son who, giggling almost uncontrollably the whole time, gave me the macho re-wrap.

There is another side to Bali, however, that stuns your senses as soon as you leave the southern tourist towns and head towards the centre and north of the island. We travelled through rural landscapes which probably had not changed much in the last thousand years. Rice is the staple crop and is grown everywhere from waterlogged lowlands to steep hillsides where ingenious irrigation systems create the emerald green terraces. Water buffalo, knee deep in mud, still patiently drag rudimentary ploughs across paddy fields and after the rice is harvested, small flocks of ducks are shepherded through to make sure no grain is wasted. In narrow, dusty village streets we often had to slow almost to a standstill while mangey dogs lethargically sniffed each other's rickety nether regions, or scratched and licked their own skinny bodies before reluctantly shuffling out of our way.

In contrast to the plodding pace of animal life, Bali's human inhabitants are a frenetic bunch, lean and wiry and not destined to enjoy the old age we take for granted in the West. We seldom saw anyone, old or young, walking or cycling, who was not carrying something. Occasionally, miles from anywhere, we might see an old man walking along beside the road carrying a plank of timber, from where and to where we had no idea. One woman elegantly balancing material or a pot of some sort on her head could meet another trudging along under the weight of a bundle of sticks or some bricks. Indeed, we saw several building sites where more women than men were sharing the backbreaking toil. Bicycles tended to be festooned from the ground up with anything from exotic fruits to plastic toilet brushes, loads stacked so precariously that the riders could only wobble gently along scarcely able to see the road ahead.

It's probably very non-PC to use the analogy of a colony of ants but that really was the image which sprung to mind when we stopped for a moment and watched the bustling people of Bali going about their business. Once, when touring up in the central mountains, we got caught by a sudden storm and took shelter in a restaurant. We sat there eating and drinking as a curtain of rain beat down on the steaming tin roof and flattened the lush gardens all around. Suddenly a huge tree, its roots perhaps weakened by the deluge, crashed across the road right outside completely blocking the way, not that any traffic was daring to move just yet. As we sat there pondering how the blocked road would affect our plans, about 20 men armed with rakes, saws, axes, brooms and chainsaws, appeared from nowhere and began demolishing the tree. Within half an hour the rain had stopped, we were ready to be on our way, and there was no sign—not a branch, a twig or even a leaf—of the fallen tree.

Bali is unusual for being a mainly Hindu island in the midst of Muslim Indonesia. There are thousands of Buddhist temples and shrines everywhere and little offerings also appear on improvised altars flanked by joss sticks in such unexpected places as doorways and even on car bonnets. Temples abound and we never failed to be impressed at how beautifully dressed people were, especially the women, who attended the frequent religious ceremonies. There is something very comforting about being in such a spiritual community. Mind you, the separation of god and mammon doesn't always work, even in Bali. We weaved our way along the coast one evening racing to catch the sunset as it bathed Tanah Lot, the famous temple perched breathtakingly on a rocky outcrop in the sea a short distance from shore. However, we found the experience much less moving than it might have been thanks to the cafes, Coke signs and other crass commercialism which now blights this serene spot.

At Ubud, the artistic, creative and almost geographic centre of Bali, we visited dozens of art, batik and carving shops. The quality of the work was astonishing and though it begged to be taken away by the

containerload we showed commendable restraint and practicality, buying only a smiling wooden mask and a large batik landscape. Later we
went to an evening of traditional Balinese dance at Ubud Palace where
the audience was held spellbound by the expressive eye, head and finger movements of the beautiful doll-like dancers. Next day we pressed
on to Singarajah, the old capital, with its sprawling, spice-laden market, and finally to Bedugul, cool and refreshing in the mountain air.
We arrived just on dark when all that was left were fairly basic cabins,
but in the morning we were amply compensated with a spectacular
view of mist rising off Lake Bratan. That night in the communal eating
hall everyone gathered round the television. As usual in Bali it was
tuned to some extremely noisy, '70s-style kung-fu programme, with
menacing cartoon baddies, shapely manacled blonde goodies, and
plenty of graphic sound effects in the fight scenes. We couldn't understand a word so instead watched rats of a different sort scuttling about
in the rafters overhead as we ate dinner.

At our hotel in Ubud the receptionist proudly told us Mick Jagger
had stayed there during his recent visit. No, sorry, let me just re-phrase
that. She said Mick Jagger had stayed in Ubud on a recent visit but not
at this particular hotel. I'd hate to give the impression we were slum-
ming it at the sort of place frequented by one of the richest and most
famous men on the planet. After all, we're budget travellers and the
only way we might ever have stayed at the same hotel as Mick would be
if he happened to have been taken there by his parents when he was a
kid. All of which reminds me of an increasingly common practice
among tour guides: no matter whereabouts in the world, they insist
upon identifying some place along the route as belonging to a household name from the world of show business. It's almost as if it would
be a matter of unbearable community shame if they couldn't match a
film star to that particularly prominent mansion or a music celebrity to
whatever lies behind those high walls and huge electronic gates. Now I
hesitate to suggest they're just making things up, but we are beginning
to see a suspiciously large number of properties belonging to the likes

of Elton John, Tom Cruise, Sting and Madonna. From dream locations in Asia to the south of France the story is the same: "El-ton Yohn, ees a hees house."

We stood on the quay looking up at the towering, rusty hull which was to carry us to the neighbouring island of Lombok and tried hard not to recall those regular media reports of ferry disasters in this part of the world. Of course they might have been in the Philippines or the South China Sea and not Indonesia, but it was still too close for comfort—unpredictable storms, over-loaded boats, primitive safety equipment, hundreds drowned. As it turned out though, this was a perfect day for rust buckets. The sea was dead calm and we spent the four-hour crossing reading books in the sunshine and wolfing down chocolate icecreams from the boat's single cafe. At the other end we crammed into a van with five Canadians, their backpacks and all our luggage, plus three surfboards...and a maniac at the wheel. For most of the journey he was half out of his seat, turning round to chat in broken English and trying to maintain eye contact at the same time, for all the world as if someone else was driving. His seven passengers were strangely subdued. Gripping our seats and staring straight ahead into the darkness, we were mesmerised by fleeting images of cyclists, donkeys and other obstacles on the road which loomed briefly in the faint headlights as we hurtled past. After an hour or so we reached Sengigi, quietly vowing never to worry about ferries again.

We spent our first night in a grotty place where the sink leaked all over our feet and the fan sounded like a cat struggling to rid itself of a particularly gruesome fur ball. After a few hours of fitful sleep we were finally put out of our misery by the 6am call to prayers at the local mosque, a call which, accompanied by strident music, boomed across the district several times a day on a tinny amplification system. It was just the incentive we needed to set off in search of new lodgings.

We walked about two miles and eventually booked in at the least westernised accommodation we could find and afford, Santai Cottages. Here the decor was bamboo and carved wood, each cottage had a hammock swaying on the verandah, and for cooling showers in our private al fresco bathroom we had to pull the bung from an earthenware pot wedged in the fork of a tree. There was a communal library-cum-dining area where guests, mostly Germans, English and Australians, sat around on cushions at night eating vegetarian meals by lamplight. Some 20 cottages were hidden from each other by dense tropical vegetation and best of all it was only a short sandy stroll from the beach and the warm clear waters of the Lombok Strait. In other words, it was a perfect place to relax and escape the tourist traps of Bali.

Most evenings a couple of the staff would start strumming guitars and we'd sometimes sit until midnight listening to them sing sweet, mournful songs by Bob Dylan, James Taylor, the Beatles and their favourite, Bob Marley. On the night of my 49th birthday, by special request, they included *Happy Birthday To You* in the repertoire. Early each morning someone crept round the cottages leaving breakfast on every verandah, normally a flask of tea with something like fried bananas, toast and honey, fruit, and, one day, boiled eggs. Lying under a mosquito net on our huge bamboo bed we never heard breakfast arrive; but like the warm air, gentle breeze and fine sea haze, it was magically always there when we stepped outside.

We spent a fair bit of time swimming, sitting in the shade of willowy palm trees and grazing at nearby restaurants up and down the beach. Inevitably there were a few hawkers patrolling the sand, among them a scrap of a woman selling small juicy pineapples. She was short and wrinkled and would break into a cheerful toothless cackle as soon as she saw us. She looked ancient and we privately dubbed her "The Old Crone"…until the day we discovered that, despite being a grandmother, she was in fact only 44, the same age as Maria. She casually carried a razor-sharp machete with which she expertly trimmed off the pineapple skin, leaving a little tuft of leaf so it could be held upside down and eaten like an icecream cone. These things were so deliciously refreshing we rapidly became two of her best customers, though there was still the usual haggling process to go through. We finally settled close to her asking price of a few pence each and since we all knew pineapples were virtually being given away in the market, everyone was happy.

When it came time to leave Lombok we reluctantly clambered aboard a near-vintage aircraft for the 25-minute flight back to Bali's main airport at Denpasar. The plane was one of those with nothing separating the crew from the passengers who were able to watch the female co-pilot going about her skilful duties. For the first half of the journey she used a box of Kleenex to methodically dust all the dials while on the approach to Denpasar—and this was mildly unsettling—she went round again tapping every dial. However, we landed safely and after transferring to a real plane needed only three more hours in the air before the undercarriage was locking into place over Perth.

Stuck out there on a limb in Western Australia, Perth has the strange claim to fame of being perhaps the most isolated large city in the world: 2,000 miles of desert or sea separate Perth from its nearest similarly-sized neighbour. Adelaide is the closest major Australian city though Perth is actually nearer to Indonesia than to many parts of Oz. When we lived in Brisbane, on the east coast of Australia, we were closer to our home in New Zealand than to Perth. So we decided to take the opportunity to visit this city of over a million people knowing we weren't likely to be in the neighbourhood again for a while. We also had plans to catch up with a former nursing buddy of Maria's who had emigrated from Blenheim a few years before. It turned out she was making a name for herself in a highly specialised branch of nursing care so, combining business with pleasure, I roped her in as an excellent subject for another of my newspaper features.

We had been to Australia before on a six-week holiday so knew parts of this vast country which, in many respects, is similar to New Zealand. After Indonesia it was reassuring in lots of ways to be back in familiar territory…just simple things which we usually take for granted like taps and lights that work, being able to read a newspaper, drink the water, recognise food in the shops and know everyone speaks English. We spent the next few days exploring Perth which is rightly renowned for its sun, sand and surf. It also turned out to have plenty of parks, squares and shops, a scattering of fine old buildings, a wonderful library and almost unlimited cafes, restaurants and bars.

One afternoon we took a train 12 miles along the coast to Freemantle. This pretty little port town received the mother of all makeovers when it hosted the America's Cup yacht race in 1987 and today, long after the circus has left town, local residents and visitors alike continue to reap the benefits. Along with the injection of cash came an Everest of positive worldwide publicity as the Aussies defended the cup they had won four years before in the States. On that occasion the whole sports-mad nation had rejoiced as *Australia II* wrenched the prize from American hands for the first time in 132 years. Unfortunately though in the 1987 Freemantle defence the Aussies couldn't hang on to the silverware and the Yanks took the trophy home again. In the interests of fairness, to say nothing of the good-natured trans-Tasman rivalry between Australia and New Zealand, it's worth noting that the Kiwis have since won AND successfully defended the cup.

Since we set out on our travels one of our main priorities has been to keep in regular touch with our children, other family members and friends. It hasn't always been easy, or cheap, but as time goes on we're becoming much cleverer with our communications. Initially we armed ourselves with New Zealand Telecom cards which we could use anywhere in the world with the charges magically appearing weeks later on our Visa statements. That worked well but like other phone cards we've used since in England and Australia, it proved an expensive way to keep in touch. Since then either we've grown smarter or, more likely, the phone companies have become super-competitive because we've now hooked into systems giving us international calls for virtually the same price as domestic dialling.

During our first year on the road we would occasionally find somewhere to type long letters, photocopy them and fire them off to family and friends. In addition, we've always been huge fans of postcards which we tend to scoop up by the fistful and send periodically in batches of 20 or 30 as we blitz through our address books. But without doubt the greatest way to keep in touch, especially given our nomadic lifestyle, is e-mail.

Back in New Zealand after 12 months away we bought a second-hand laptop which now goes everywhere with us. It was originally intended as a convenient writing tool for my work but very soon, via simple Internet connections and e-mail, it became a means of keeping in touch with almost anyone, anywhere, any time. For speed and convenience it takes some beating, and it's also cheap enough, though being budget travellers we are always sniffing out ways to make it even cheaper. Occasionally we have had to bite the bullet and fork out at Internet cafes or at some libraries and hostels where they charge for computer time. But more often than not we have ferreted out the freebies. In America and Australia this has proved remarkably easy with university and college facilities generally bristling with easy-access on-line terminals. Similarly most public libraries in those countries—and slowly this now seems to be spreading to England—happily provide free Internet access though reasonably enough they often have a booking system and a time limit.

Receiving mail from home—electronic or snail, it doesn't matter—is always cause for celebration. Before leaving New Zealand we arranged for our post to be re-directed to Bob and once we settle somewhere we contact him with our new forwarding address. That's the theory. In practice it has never worked quite so smoothly. Like orbiting space ships, some of our mail seems to circle the world many times before coming in to land; other items simply go AWOL for anything up to six months before appearing out of nowhere; sadly a few bits of post are still missing in action, feared irretrievably lost down the back of the Great Sorting Machine in the Sky. Because we are constantly on the move, e-mail has proved the most dependable means of communication and signing in to our Hotmail address several times a week still gives us a buzz. However, electronic junk mail has become a real pain, especially since living in the States. Daily we are bombarded by "great new offers" for loans, insurance, dental plans, travel, college degrees, cars, girls with big chests, and much much more. We block the sender's address on every piece of junk that lands but it's a Canute-like exercise in futility…only the delete button can hold back this tide.

The trouble with travelling in countries like Indonesia, where things are so much cheaper, is that you end up spending a lot more money than you ever intended. It's one of those unfathomable little laws about money, like the one which says no matter how much you earn, you're always broke at the end of the week/month/year. Sure enough by the time we got to Perth our cash reserves were low and our credit card balance was high.

When we lived in Blenheim, Maria and I were both involved in various clubs and community groups and, inevitably, were on numerous committees. It's with this background in mind that from time to time we jokingly call meetings of our own "finance committee" which, of course, has just two members. Such meetings, usually precipitated by the arrival of bank statements or large bills, are the signal to grab pen and paper and have a stab at assessing just where we stand: how much money have we got, what bills have to be paid, when's the mortgage due, how close we are to our bank limits, and what "ships" may be bobbing around on the horizon bringing funds in our general direction. I suppose every household goes through something similar but in our case this exercise can become quite complicated. For example, at times we have had credit cards, cash cards and bank accounts in New Zealand, Australia, England and the United States. Okay, so hardly the sort of high finance to send rivulets of sweat coursing from a Rothschild armpit but still a challenge for those of us who only just scraped O level maths. We have also had to file tax returns in all those countries, but that's another story…

By now, some six months after quitting the workforce in New Zealand, it was definitely time to return to proper jobs and start earning regular money again, if only to give our friendly bank manager back in Blenheim a decent night's sleep. Our plan all along was to settle for a while in Melbourne and do just that, though I don't think either of us realised quite how difficult it would be. Maria found agency work almost at once but it was stressful as she was being moved to different nursing situations and locations almost daily and had to travel long distances by tram and bus around the sprawling city. In my case it was several weeks and around 50 rejection letters before I found myself working two unskilled and low paid jobs. At the same time we had problems finding accommodation and, after two weeks cramped in very small youth hostel rooms, ended up in a flat which wasn't anything to write home about. Because of all these hassles Melbourne probably marks the low point in our travels to date, but for all that we wouldn't have missed the chance to spend a long, hot summer in this most vibrant of cities.

Each time we go to live and work in a new country it's incredibly exciting and stimulating but it also brings unexpected stresses and strains. It's a bit like condensing a whole lifetime into just six months or a year. You arrive, you don't know anyone, you have to find your way around a completely new environment, you must arrange official things like bank accounts and tax numbers, you have to find a job, buy a car, find somewhere to live. Then, a matter of months later, you start to unpick everything—give in your notice at work, say goodbye to new-found friends, sell the car, clean the flat, move out and reclaim your bond, arrange to have mail sent on, pay final utility bills, close bank accounts, and finally pack up everything you possess, jump on a plane to somewhere new and do it all over again. Exhilarating and, yes, it does get easier each time, but still not for the faint-hearted.

For some months I had been hoping—unrealistically as it turned out—for a job on the *Melbourne Age* newspaper. I had contacts there, had sent my CV, written several letters and made numerous phone calls. But our arrival in the Victorian capital coincided with some major retrenchment in the local media industry and the place was awash with jobless journos. So instead of writing for the *Age*, I found myself poring over the paper's "sits vac" columns and firing off salvos of job applications. I tried anything connected to the media, advertising, marketing or public relations, and when that didn't work I widened the net to include office work, driving, warehouse jobs and just about anything else the employment agencies had on their books.

I hadn't been job-hunting like this since leaving Liverpool University in the late '60s when, the ink hardly dry on my degree, I had been pretty much able to pick and choose what I wanted. Thirty years later it was a rude shock to find the rules of the game had changed radically. My days became largely dominated by the search for work—writing job application letters, photocopying my CV, references and clippings, and posting everything off in huge envelopes. In most cases I never even received a reply, which seemed bloody rude, or else an ad ran in the paper weeks later thanking me and maybe a hundred others for our interest and informing us the position had now been filled. I did have a couple of interviews and, quite early on, the offer of a job as a glorified filing clerk for a technical publishing company. The pay was terrible and when I asked to start a little higher up the scale they backed off and gave the job to someone else. At the time I didn't really mind. It was still early days and I was full of optimism that something better would come along. But after a few more fruitless weeks I came to the sombre realisation that a bird in the hand is worth a hundred advertised in the "sits vac".

Melbourne's new Crown Casino was another avenue I explored. They were busy recruiting hundreds of staff so I applied to become a croupier and attended the marathon four-hour interviewing process. This began with a briefing followed by tests to establish a psychological profile, lots of self analysis stuff, IQ tests, English and maths. At times I wondered if I was in the right room or had inadvertently strayed into the entrance exam for something rather more cerebral like the diplomatic service. Anyway, I got through it all okay but then discovered I would have to wait at least a month before I could begin the necessary four weeks of unpaid training, and I didn't relish the prospect of another two months with no income. One reason the job appealed in the first place was because I thought it could lead to work on cruise ships which was something we have long been interested in. I certainly had no desire to spend my days and nights in casinos which, while okay for brief visits, generally strike me as awful, unhealthy places with their pervasive atmosphere of sad desperation.

During this time I had also been writing my features and sending them, with photos, to various newspapers around New Zealand and to some in Australia. By good fortune I stumbled into the Royal Melbourne Institute of Technology on only our second day in the city and discovered they had a journalism department. I talked to one of the tutors and managed to bluff my way into using their computers and other facilities to write my stories. Soon I was quietly beavering away in one corner, turning out my stories, writing my job applications and making full use of the copier and coffee machines in the staff room on the floor below. Of course it was too good to last. After about 10 days a rather butch woman, who appeared to have two recently watered shrubberies growing in her armpits, backed me against a wall (gulp) and politely but firmly pointed out the facilities were for journalism students only. However, I only had to walk about 50 yards across campus to find my next "office", a computer lab where I was warmly welcomed and given free access to any of the 50-plus terminals, provided no students were waiting. By now it was early December and most self-respecting students were in summer vacation mode; hoards of sweaty, book-laden, terribly intense and anxious looking young people shuffling around behind my seat would not become a problem for another three months.

At the same time as job-hunting we were frantically searching for a flat, desperate to escape the increasingly claustrophobic youth hostel. Rental accommodation in Melbourne was at a premium with little about, at least in our price range, and huge demand fuelled by the burgeoning student population. This classic supply and demand imbalance meant people would be queuing up when local estate agents handed out their weekly rental lists and places would be snapped up often before we even had a chance to view them. Another complication was that most landlords rented for a minimum of a year whereas we wanted only a six-month lease.

Our luck finally changed when we found a ground-floor flat in a modern block owned by the Royal Melbourne Hospital. It was brilliantly located in North Melbourne, close to the hospital, the university and Victoria Market, and well within walking distance of the city centre and areas like Lygon Street, famed for its Italian restaurants, cake shops and other eateries. The flat was unfurnished but we didn't want the hassle of buying stuff, carting it around and then having to sell it again in six months. So first stop was a furniture hire centre where, in a special deal for $35 per week, we got a double bed, dining table and six chairs, two couches, a chest of drawers, two bedside cabinets and a large corner unit—pretty much the line-up American motorists have to swerve around on the average commute to work.

A few trips to Victoria Market—an amazing place selling everything from shoes to live chickens—and various discount stores yielded such necessities as linen, duvets, a mirror, crockery and cutlery. We got everything else, including a single bed, hoover, desk and chair, even more cheaply after rummaging through the contents of several student flats advertised in "For Sale" notices plastered around the university. All those bits and pieces we eventually sold on in one job lot to the next tenants when we moved out. Our flat wasn't great compared to some of the places we've rented since. But after six months virtually living out of suitcases it was lovely to have a base again, somewhere we could unpack everything and even hang up our little New Zealand flag.

All this time Maria had been working her socks off. Within four days of arriving in Melbourne she had had an interview with a nursing agency, been given a uniform and a bleeper, and was out there ministering to the sick and needy. She was working shifts, some days starting as early as 6.30am and other days not finishing until 11pm. The pay was pretty good, especially at weekends when she was biting chunks out of our credit card debt at the rate of $35 an hour. However, she rarely seemed to go to the same hospital or clinic two days running so was always under the extra pressure of having to work in different places, with different staff, different systems and different ways of doing things. It was only after she nailed down a job at the Royal Melbourne, just a five-minute walk from our flat, that her days of crazy commuting finally came to an end.

Melbourne, home to more than three million people, sprawls out in all directions as if it had been dropped from a great height. It took us a while to get to grips with just how big it all is and we soon realised looking at maps was hopeless. What seemed just a few streets and at most a leisurely half-hour journey between our flat and where Maria was working turned out to be a nightmare two-hour round trip featuring a 40-minute rattling, swaying tram ride followed by a 10-minute jog and a final 500-yard sprint to make it on time. One scorching Sunday afternoon Maria was finishing work on yet another new ward at 3pm and I thought it would be fun to walk back with her. Because it was such a hot day I left plenty of time for a gentle stroll but I began to quicken my pace a little after asking several people how far the hospital was and each time being advised to catch a bus. I was sweating buckets by now and would gladly have taken their advice but on Sunday afternoons buses were few and far between. In the end I started running and reached the hospital about five past three, puce and panting like a St Bernard in a sauna, only to find Maria had got a lift home. She was there relaxing with a cold drink when I staggered in dusty and dehydrated almost three hours later.

Meanwhile, I had lowered my job sights considerably and started applying for almost anything just to help bring in a little more cash. So it was I began my short-lived career as a dog food telemarketer. The company I joined had a squad of people going door-to-door giving out free samples of dog food. Those who took the bait agreed to a follow-up call a few days later and I was part of the team making those calls.

The aim was to persuade people to place orders and it was a joy to watch Jeremy, the young smoothie in charge of the sales team, reeling in the customers. I tried to follow his example but my technique was seriously flawed. However, at $15 an hour I resolved to give it my best shot.

It didn't help that I was interviewed on Monday and started on Tuesday without training or even a briefing; everything I knew about the company and its product I'd read in their brochure on the bus home. The first evening I worked through about 30 calls, got lots of very positive feedback from happy dog owners, but no sales. The second night I upped my rate to about 45 calls. Still no luck though I took heart from the fact that a much more experienced woman working alongside me scored only one firm order during the shift. At the same time though I sensed Jeremy was having doubts about my elaborately embroidered but largely fictitious exploits as a salesman and sure enough he phoned a couple of days later to say the company was trying a different approach and blah, blah, blah, my cheque was in the post. But there must be money in dog food…some time after Christmas I was back in the business with another fledgling company, this time delivering the stuff by van all over Melbourne.

There was an added emotional dimension to our first Christmas away from home and it was lovely that the kids were flying across the Tasman to join us. We had long since arranged their trips using our frequent flyer points and it was marvellous to see them both again for the first time in six months. William arrived on December 13 and Emma, having just finished her fourth year veterinary exams, came one week later. William at this stage had dropped out of university after a couple of years, done a year at jazz school and was now playing bass guitar in a band in Christchurch. He was, how can I put this? Rebelling? Revolting? Yes, that's more like it. He and his mates either shaved their heads or sported mohawk strips down the centre; they wore filthy, tattered old clothes, one of the favourite fashion statements being a combo of thermal underwear and heavy Doc Martin-type boots. At the time William was part of the transient population in a flat-from-hell dubbed Kaos by those living there. Some people might describe all this as going through a phase though the overall impression was more of going through a hedge backwards. Consequently, it was not altogether a surprise when we had to wait ages at the airport while he was frisked by officials after being fingered by one of the trained sniffer dogs. In those days bodily hygiene was not a high priority for William's crowd and having been caught downwind a few times ourselves, our sympathies were entirely with the dog.

There's no doubt Melbourne is a fantastic summer city catering for all tastes. Firstly it's a real sports mecca with events like the Australian Open tennis, international test match cricket and the Australian Grand Prix. On top of that summer brings a whole crop of special music and cultural festivals, outdoor concerts and shows, in addition to all the regular attractions at places as diverse as the spectacular arts centre and the only slightly less spectacular casino complex. With the kids there we also took the opportunity to do things like visiting a wildlife sanctuary where the attractions included some of Australia's frighteningly venomous snakes and a display featuring birds of prey in action. This was excellent, especially the way it degenerated into pure farce when one of the eagles took off and didn't come back. For quite a while afterwards the embarrassed handler stood watching the diminishing speck in the sky saying things like "Ah, here she comes" and "She'll be back when she spots this piece of tucker" and, finally, "I think that might be a male eagle up there she's seen."

5

Our house in Blenheim is called Mildura. We have never really found out why. The place just came with that name on the gate. The only other Mildura we know of is the town in Victoria whose claim to fame appears to be its sun-dried raisins which we occasionally find on supermarket shelves. Apparently local wags there say dried fruit is the town's whole raisin d'etre. Anyway, not having anywhere else particular to go, we decided to stick with tradition and have Christmas in Mildura. What we didn't appreciate at the time was just how far Mildura is from Melbourne. Once again Australian maps gave no true idea of distances and were truly deficient this time in not having the route clearly marked in bright red capital letters reading: "A f****** long way!" It wasn't until afterwards, having spent a total of 18 hours, or a quarter of our Christmas getaway, scrunched up in a hire car, that we realised just what we'd let ourselves in for.

It had the potential to be a total disaster but in the end we all had a rather good Christmas. All of us, that is, except for a number of colourful parrots along the way. Well, Maria likes to drive fast and the roads were very straight and empty, but for some reason she has a blind spot when it comes to parrots. Even vivid pink and mauve and purple and green ones.

We three passengers are all slumped in our seats, looking out for kangaroos in the flat, arid countryside, just idly chatting, when we notice something on the road about half a mile ahead. As we get closer we realise it's a flock of beautiful parrots...but Maria isn't slowing down, she's still merrily gibbering away. We all fall silent, we begin to uncurl and sit up, we make feeble flapping gestures with our arms; surely she must see them now. Thump, thump, thud, thud, thump. Suddenly the air is pink with floating feathers as if someone's been having a pillow fight in a gay bar. A few of those feathers cling desperately to our windscreen wipers before finally giving up the struggle another 100 yards down the highway. Behind us the road looks like a clip from the opening scene of the Spielberg sequel, *Saving Private Polly*. We all turn to stare in horror at the driver: "Christ Maria, didn't you see those birds!" Obviously not, for she did exactly the same thing again about three hours later. Considerably less ruffled than most of the unfortunate parrots, Maria, to her credit, does not attempt to deny the crime. But her defence is shaky, relying as it does upon feminine logic. "Well it's their fault, they should have got out of the way."

It turns out one reason they didn't is because they were likely too full of grain to move. An old farmer we met along the way to Mildura told us how the birds flock to the roadway to feed on grain spilt from passing trucks. It's an easy meal but, as with humans, over indulging carries certain health risks. The old boy we were talking to and his wife had almost given up trying to make a living farming in the harsh landscape of central Victoria and now supplemented their income by running a petrol station with a little cafe and shop attached. We were incredibly lucky to find them. We had set off on Christmas Day just expecting there would be plenty of enterprising Shell and BP service station owners out to make a killing from the holiday traffic. What traffic? The route was deserted…no traffic, no service stations, and apart from Ballarat almost no towns. The needle was beyond E and the little light was flashing insistently when, following the directions of residents in the nearest town, we eventually found this place. Oh what joy! What wonderful Christmas presents! A tank of petrol, sandwiches, cakes, cups of tea and cold drinks, just when we thought we were going to spend Christmas Day stuck in the middle of nowhere. Of course, when we finally reached Mildura we realised we were stuck in the middle of nowhere.

Mildura is a fair-sized town but there is just nothing there. Well, maybe a giant, five-storey, fibreglass raisin by the side of the road, I can't remember. In steady rain—the first they'd had in four months—we wandered around the deserted town and then back to our motel. We were all pretty tired and heading for early nights but first we pulled our crackers, put on our silly paper hats and celebrated with a non-traditional Christmas dinner of mushroom omelette. We woke to clear sunny skies and spent Boxing Day morning cruising along the mighty Murray River on a paddle steamer. Hoping for lunch we drove out to a couple of wineries but they were closed, the owners probably enjoying Christmas somewhere with friends who run service stations. Still, it didn't matter to us. It was hot again by now so we made our way back to the motel, ate and drank, swam in the pool, and flopped with our books and magazines. It was a lovely restful day which was just what we needed…we had a long drive back ahead of us.

Emma and William were still with us for New Year's Eve so we joined thousands of people packing the streets down by the Yarra River to watch fireworks and welcome in 1997. Over the next few days we squeezed in a few more Melbourne outings though unfortunately both had gone back to New Zealand by the start of the Australian Open. Maria and I sweltered through one of the opening days but it was well worth it to see both eventual champions in action, Pete Sampras and Martina Hingis. Even though we were miles up in the stands we even got a rather good action photo of the hairy Sampras torso caught in mid serve. It wasn't just heating up on court—later that same week raging bush fires destroyed homes in the Dandenongs, a beautiful but tinder-dry wooded range within easy commuting distance of the city.

The signs were there for those who could read them…Melbourne was heading for a long, hot summer of record temperatures. It was the summer when swimming pools stayed open all night and were kept busy with people who couldn't sleep because of the heat; when at the end of the television news one night the staid and suited weatherman suddenly surprised viewers and his colleagues in the studio by picking up a glass of water and pouring it over himself. It was perfect weather to be sitting in a cool air-conditioned office somewhere. Shame I wasn't doing that. Instead, with the mercury often bubbling around

40C, I found myself enjoying and enduring my most physically active summer in 30 years.

After the long work drought I landed two jobs within a couple of weeks: door-to-door market research and delivering dog food. At first the market research surveys were only at weekends and even when a few other odd days were thrown in it still seemed I could easily manage the half-time driving job as well. However, more and more survey work kept coming my way and before long keeping both jobs going meant I was flat out six days a week. All of which helped pay the rent while the unaccustomed exercise was great for my waistline but it didn't leave Maria and I much time together. One day a week, in fact, which brought back memories of those American summer camps.

Doing market research surveys I was constantly amazed at how trusting people can be. They would welcome me, a complete stranger, into their homes, offer me a cool drink and happily give me up to an hour of their valuable weekends or evenings. Not only that, but many would quite cheerfully allow me to scribble down all sorts of information about their personal and financial affairs; questions I was sometimes quite embarrassed to ask, they would answer without batting an eyelid. I was working for AGB McNair, one of the major market research companies, at least in Australia and New Zealand. My first assignment ran at weekends and was a very detailed lifestyle questionnaire called Panorama, presumably so named because it covered such a wide range of topics. Much of it involved repetitive questions about newspaper and magazine readership, while there were other sections on things like television and travel, and always the personal demographic stuff—age, education, marital status, family details, income and so on.

There were two things I quickly learned going door-to-door. The first was that the vast majority of people would never dream of answering a survey and I quickly got used to refusals varying between the polite "No thank you" and the more pointed "Piss off mate". The second thing was that the first thing didn't matter because there are also plenty of other people who will bend over backwards to help you. The trick is finding them and only way to do that is to knock on as many doors as you have to, as quickly as you can. Most of the market research was paid on an hourly basis but Panorama and its companion survey Omnibus were at a set rate. Ten interviews were needed and if you hit a good streak and knocked them all off in one day, as I managed to do a couple of times, the hourly rate looked pretty handsome; more often it took most of the weekend, so the pay scale became somewhat less impressive.

In case you're thinking 10 interviews doesn't sound much there was another catch, a quota system, which meant we were only allowed certain numbers of males and females in each age group. What this often came down to was, at the end of another stinking hot day, with just one more interview needed, a lovely, friendly and very cooperative young woman would answer the door. I would run through some preliminary questions and be on the point of believing there really is a God after all when I'd ask her age. She's 22 and to fill my quota I need someone in the 25–30 range. On such occasions it was terribly tempting to fiddle the books and I must confess once in a while I succumbed to the theory that the easiest way to overcome temptation is to give into it.

As I was allocated additional surveys, the work gradually slipped into a monotonous pattern of long, hot, dry, dusty days pounding suburban pavements. To reach these areas I had to take public transport, usually the bus. One memorably hot Saturday the city's Met buses were on strike so I had to walk an hour before even starting my rounds. That was bad enough but when I rounded the last bend I was really pissed off to find three buses waiting. It turned out this was not a Met route and these drivers were working as normal. I had to slavishly follow little grid maps marking my area, call at every single house and complete reams of paperwork—increasingly stained with sweat and suncream as the day wore on—both during the survey and at the end of each session. I used to start at 9am carrying a two-litre bottle of frozen water in my backpack. By 10 o'clock it would all be melted, and by 11 o'clock it would all be gone.

I couldn't help noticing some people at McNair's were given product-testing surveys which meant they were able to hand out little sample packs of everything from tuna, chocolate biscuits and cereal, to drinks and cosmetics. Hand them out and hang on to a few for themselves by all accounts. These appeared to be closely guarded plum jobs almost reverentially passed down from father to son. Despite constantly volunteering my services, the nearest I ever got to this freebie heaven was staggering around Melbourne with two backpacks containing 20 kilograms of washing powder. I was supposed to be finding suitable guinea pigs to test this wonderful new product and tell us what they thought of the smell. However, it proved a particularly frustrating assignment because while plenty of people were willing to help us, a ridiculously restrictive preliminary screening survey ruled out 99.9 percent of them. Maria and I kept finding soap powder in the cracks and crevices of those backpacks for months afterwards.

As the weeks wore on, one thing I came to enjoy about market research was the variety. I had a couple of what they called "intercept" surveys where we hovered around and grabbed people at particular locations. One was at the Moomba Festival, one of the late summer's most spectacular all-round family entertainment events; the other was outside a liquor store. For several extremely easy and lucrative days I was part of a team measuring the amount of space goods were taking up on the shelves of a new supermarket. We measured spaces, called out bar codes, the information was all fed into a laptop computer and nobody seemed to know quite why. There was a city council survey seeking feedback on proposals for a park redevelopment, and another project recruiting people for a representative nationwide sample of consumers who were asked to monitor and record all their shopping.

But perhaps the most unusual job of all was as a mystery shopper—I had to pose as a potential new-car buyer and secretly report on the performance of the car dealership. I had to rate them on everything from

the layout and appearance of the showrooms to things like how technical the salesman's presentation was, if they offered me a test drive (no)
and whether they gave me a follow-up call (yes). In many respects they
were dreadful. For example, they ignored me for ages when I first
arrived and during this time I could clearly hear a couple of salesmen
trading obscenities in one of the offices. Then while sitting at a desk
being briefed by a salesman he broke off in mid-presentation to take an
obviously routine domestic phone call from his wife. Boy, I enjoyed
writing that report.

If it was hot outside during that Melbourne summer it was a hell of
a lot hotter inside the oven on wheels which doubled as the dog food
delivery van. It was an enclosed van with just two sliding windows at
the front, a cooling system that didn't work and an engine blasting out
much-appreciated additional heat and fumes a couple of inches below
my backside. During the day, as the outside temperatures soared,
inside the van it reached the stage where jumping down into the blaz-
ing sun and sprinting up pathways weighed down with heavy bags or
tins of dog food had a strangely cooling effect.

This was a shoestring start-up company operating out of a warehouse in Richmond, not far from the city centre. The pay stank and so
did the warehouse, mainly thanks to Oliver, a comical little French
bulldog puppy with an over-active bowel and bladder, who belonged
to the boss and consequently spent long hours on site. David, who had
been a stockbroker, financial advisor and farmer in his previous lives,
was the entrepreneur behind the business which he was hoping to
build up and then either franchise or sell. Working for him he had a
coterie of office and sales staff, a dour full-time driver called Bruce and
two part-time drivers, myself and another bloke I didn't meet but who
one day called in sick with heat stroke and never returned. The dog
food, trucked from a factory somewhere in up-state Victoria, was
touted as being particularly healthy compared to the rubbish found in
supermarkets. There were a number of different canned meals, several

of which featured trendy combinations of rice and vegetables, plus two or three sorts of dry food.

I spent my first day out on the road with Bruce who was nut brown, lean as a whippet and claimed to be an ex-postie. I say "claimed" because by the end of the first day I was convinced he was either some sort of extra-terrestrial being or at the very least an android. We hit the road around 8am and finished a roasting nine and a half hours later. During that whole time Bruce was either driving or running. He ran up to houses carrying dog food, he ran back. He didn't stop to eat, drink or go to the loo. In fact the only concession he made to the day's 38C was at one property where he jogged to the garden hose, took a few sips and sprinkled some water round the back of his neck. Obviously a couple of his circuits must have been malfunctioning at the time.

It didn't take long for me to realise Bruce was not showing off for my benefit. The man was a machine. Every day he was at work before me packing up orders and loading both vans. He usually had more deliveries to make than me, left later, still got back sooner and would invariably be wading through the next day's orders by the time I trailed in. In the four months I did this job I could count the number of times I got back to the warehouse before Bruce on the fingers of a two-toed sloth. We tended to deliver mostly in the far suburbs and some days I drove almost 20 miles out of the city before my first drop-off. I had a disintegrating *Melway* in the van, a detailed A to Z street map of Melbourne, which I had to refer to constantly. With full loads and particularly distant delivery routes, it was not unusual for my dog days to last nine or 10 hours. In fact my longest day was 10 1/2 hours during which I drove 125 miles and made 87 deliveries.

In an effort to make each trip flow as quickly and logically as possible, the van was carefully stacked and loaded according to the delivery dockets so the first drop-offs were right by the rear door and the last ones just behind the driving seat. However, some semi-rural routes way out on the city boundary had such steep hills that, even driving up as carefully as possible, I would hear the sickening sound of everything in the van shifting and tumbling about. I knew then it was going to be one of those days where, for the rest of the journey, I'd have to scramble in to the van at each stop and rummage around for the orders like a hyperactive truffle pig. However, as the weeks rolled by I began to remember the routes, master all the various short cuts and become a lot faster; a few times I even got back early enough to join Bruce and David in the excitement of packing up the next day's orders.

Driving around Melbourne gave me a better grasp of just how spread out the place was. At times on my delivery run I'd catch sight of the towering city skyline from different points maybe 10 to 15 miles away and it always looked absolutely dazzling. In places along my routes the suburbs became air brushed into the bush and it was not uncommon to see pockets of parrots and other colourful wildlife. One memorable day, just above my head in a small wattle tree, I saw (but mostly heard) a flock of magnificent snow-white cockatoos. Lovely birds but very destructive and that terrible screeching.

Considering the size of the surrounding metropolis, the city centre seemed relatively compact and accessible. Luckily I had to travel only four stops by train to reach work but the journey equated to a mini tour of Melbourne highlights. We'd rattle past the city's highest building, the Rialto Towers and alongside the Yarra River on the opposite side to the new casino which opened while we were there. To counter their legions of strident critics, the casino promoters had included in the complex loads of restaurants, expensive shops and other "entertainment" to help create the illusion this was some sort of family fun park. We went along for a nosy soon afterwards and found it very glitzy and mostly pretty tacky though some small touches like the lighting and fountains were quite impressive. From my commuting seat I could also see the old casino building with its giant billboard siren tempting punters in with the lure of winning new cars—the tally of lucky winners stood at 260 when I last looked.

The train carried on through the ornate arches of Flinders Street railway station, in the fleeting gaps between trees we'd catch a glimpse Government House, and then pass close by two of the city's major sports venues—Melbourne Park, home of the Australian Open tennis, and the famed MCG (Melbourne Cricket Ground), associated as much with Aussie Rules Football as with cricket. We attended a Rules game once. Sitting way up in the rafters we could hardly see, much less understand, the frenetic action down on the pitch but still loved the exciting atmosphere and being part of such a passionate crowd. On another occasion we took a tour of the MCG which included being allowed to walk on the hallowed turf. We filed out with our guide and stared awestruck into the towering empty stands, sensing for just a second what it must be like for our modern day sporting gladiators when they enter the arena. My daily train tour was excellent value for only the $1.40 price of a ticket, and on still mornings a balloon would often drift overhead just to add a touch of magic.

One of the most amazing and inescapable things about Melbourne is the cultural, ethnic and racial mix. The city is truly a melting pot and while this obviously has brought some problems, the overall impression we gained was of a happy, harmonious, cosmopolitan family. Anyone anxious about the effects of immigration on their country could do worse than live in Melbourne for a while to have their fears laid to rest. There are huge numbers of Italians and Greeks—Melbourne is said to have the second highest Greek population of any city in the world after Athens—plus a significant Asian population, especially Chinese and Vietnamese. Sometimes when I was working at the Institute of Technology I would glance around and notice I was the only non-Asian in the crowded computer laboratory. Similarly Maria and I were taking a train out to the suburbs one afternoon and had the carriage to ourselves before at one stop it suddenly filled completely with chattering Asian schoolgirls. Greeks, Italians, Asians and a host of other nationalities have brought their languages, cultures, food and traditions which together make this such an enriching and pulsating place to live.

What is astonishing, however, is the generational divide within these immigrant groups. Some of the older people have barely assimilated and after maybe 20 or 30 years still cannot speak English while their kids are right little Aussies. Maria often found herself dealing with patients in hospital who could not speak English. Indeed, they had never needed to since arriving in Australia; they could quite easily live, work and shop within mini communities of their own people. Maria had either to find someone to act as interpreter or make use of little translation cards at the foot of the bed which carried a number of key words and phrases in a variety of languages. I came across the same thing while doing market research. Often the person who came to the door couldn't understand or answer the simplest of questions and would call to someone else in the house for help. Invariably this would be a child, often as young as five or six, fluent in at least two languages, who would act as interpreter, their English as fair dinkum Aussie as anything you're likely to hear on *Neighbours*.

We certainly made the most of Melbourne's wonderful restaurants, food shops and markets. At least one or two nights a week we would eat out, usually in Lygon Street, usually Italian and usually sitting outside at a pavement cafe soaking up the warm evening air and people-watching. Lygon Street was an easy walk from our flat but if we had had a hard day or we were just feeling lazy we often got no further than the Eldorado, a restaurant and bar just around the corner from our place. We could probably have resisted their corny marketing motto—"Where there's a pot of gold every day of the week"—but not the great Thai and seafood snacks. And that really was the bottom line in Melbourne, indeed in the whole of Australia: the food was just so good and so reasonably priced, even for budget travellers like us. When feeling in a particularly extravagant or wicked mood we would pop in to Brunetti's, an expensive but exquisite little bakery and cake shop just off Lygon St. A note behind the counter there reads: "No chocolate kept on these premises overnight." I don't know if that is really a joke as the cakes and other goodies there are easily delicious enough to tempt any appreciative, sweet-toothed burglar.

Once we were both working in Melbourne we began planning our days off and spare evenings to make the most of our limited free time. We took day trips to places like Williamstown, a quaint and historic little town just a ferry ride across the bay from Melbourne, and the seaside suburb of St Kilda, with more tempting cake shops and baking hot sands. We actually spent Easter Sunday there, eating Easter eggs and washing them down with hot tea in a cafe at the end of the pier. We usually arrange our own travel independently, having had quite a bit of practice, but we did join a one-day bus tour to Sorrento, a well-heeled retreat almost 60 miles around the bay coast from Melbourne. The day also included a visit to the wartime gun fortifications on a finger of land called Point Nepean and to a cattle farm. There we all hungrily devoured Devonshire teas while watching kangaroos and wombats, a rather incongruous mix not commonly found in Devon.

While in Melbourne we tried to pack in as much of the entertainment on offer as possible, including indoor and outdoor concerts, art exhibitions, comedy shows and masses of movies. We also saw several plays, usually squeezing into matinee performances to stretch our dollars further. One of these afternoon shows was *Sylvia*, a charming and very funny play about a man who falls in love with a stray dog. This comedy rang lots of familiar doggy bells, was entirely appropriate for a couple of Animal Aunts and is highly recommended for all other dotty dog lovers.

In addition to everything else which used to slow me up on my dog food delivery runs, I quite frequently managed to become hopelessly lost, even with the map. Naturally I never mentioned that to Maria...no point in just handing her ammunition. Considering how much time we've spent closeted together since we started travelling—much more than we did in our previous life back in New Zealand—we have got along incredibly well. Not all the time, of course. Occasionally we start to twang each other's nerves and have a good odd spat, usually over something quite trivial. But that seems a small price to pay considering all the benefits and extra fun to be had travelling with a friend or partner compared to doing it alone. Our major bust-ups invariably happen in the car and most commonly when we are hurrying to get somewhere and lose our way.

I'm sure Maria won't mind me saying this, but it's always her fault. Not only does she get us lost but she hates to admit it and ask someone for directions. Of course we always have to ask eventually, one or other of us striding into a shop or garage or collaring some luckless pedestrian, getting the directions and, a couple of turns later, becoming completely lost again and even more angry than before. We have now developed a strategy where we both jump out and, sticking close like a couple of Mormon elders, listen to the directions together. Even this doesn't always work. Sometimes we get back in the car and can't agree if the first instruction was turn left or right. Or if it was left, did he mean here or at the end of this road? By then, of course, it doesn't much matter as we're both giggling so much we can't drive anyway.

In every marriage there are little areas where neither partner likes to tread unless they are seriously looking for one of those knock 'em down, drag 'em out, major blood letting sort of discussions. Those are the ones we most often have while driving together. Surprising how easily they start…an innocent remark about your beloved driving too fast or too slow, missing a turn or being in the wrong lane at a roundabout, and it's a re-run of Ghengis Khan's greatest hits. Maria's opening gambit is usually to pull out into the fast lane, coax the needle up to 100 and ask tight-lipped: "Do you want to drive?" I've found there's no really safe answer to that one. I tried "yes" once and the rest of the journey resembled a two-hour driving test with every gear change, indicator flash and rear mirror peek under intense scrutiny. "No, you carry on" is a marginally better bet, inviting only the flinty and ambiguous retort "Fine" followed by deep-frozen shoulder just in case I mistakenly really did think things were fine. I like to believe my own response to any spousal criticism is a lot more considered and mature.

As seismologists the world over gently put down their coffee cups and crane forward to stare in disbelief at their screens, I slam on the brakes, wrench open my door and leap out shouting: "Right, you bloody well drive then."

On the last day of May, with our round-the-world ticket nearing its critical use-by date, we left Melbourne and flew to New Zealand. After a year away it was both strange and exhilarating to be back. Strange to see everything through slightly different eyes now, in some ways more critical, in others more appreciative. And definitely exhilarating as we embarked on what amounted to a 17-day royal tour, feted by all our friends and at every turn eating and drinking far too much. In amongst all this pampering and partying we caught up with the kids again, checked that everything was well with our house and tenants, and saw our dear old dog. Buffy was remarkably happy and settled which wasn't really a surprise considering he had gone to two of the kindest people we know. But we didn't realise they were also completely daft and were spoiling him rotten; I mean, honestly, a paddling pool for Christmas and all our postcards to him tacked up inside his kennel?

We soon found we were spending a lot more time talking to a lot more people than we had planned. Partly it was because people were genuinely interested to hear about our adventures; partly it was probably because we talked too much and insisted on flashing our photo albums. Blenheim is one of those small, friendly towns where popping into the supermarket for bread and milk can easily turn into a chat-fest with a dozen different people followed by all sorts of unexpected but delightful social invitations. To be honest though, a few people didn't even know we'd been away. "Haven't seen you around for a while," said one of our son's former teachers. "Been on holiday?" All this returning home stuff was physically tiring but above all emotionally draining, and after a couple of weeks back we were starting to feel pretty fragile. We also began to panic that we might not have enough time to do all the things we wanted, so one thing we made sure of was dropping in at our old workplaces. We were both warmly greeted by former colleagues, met new faces on the team and enjoyed catching up on a year's news and gossip in under an hour. Both of us were assured of jobs if we wanted to come back, though after listening to a few tales of doom and gloom, plus a dollop of the same old office politics, it wasn't such an enticing prospect. One day, maybe.

Besides the socialising, we had to wade through a fair amount of official business, shuffling like refugees with a year's worth of paperwork between the bank manager, our accountant and the tax man, with side trips to the local council and our insurance company. At this stage there was a question mark over our tax status and whether we should continue to be considered New Zealand residents for tax purposes. This turned out to be about as grey an area as you could hope to find in a pitch-black room full of taxation lawyers. We were bombarded with well-intentioned but conflicting advice and the situation has really only resolved itself with the passing of time. Once it became clear we would be away from New Zealand for considerably longer than a couple of years, logic dictated—and the tax authorities agreed—that we should no longer be treated as residents. Naturally we also caught up with Bob during this fleeting visit home. He had continued to look after our property affairs with a degree of care and attention to detail which went well beyond the call of duty and far beyond what we could ever expect for the meagre monthly fee we were paying him. Brushing aside his protests we increased the payment and took him and his equally helpful wife Junella out for a "thank you" dinner.

It was an interesting exercise to sit down at the end of that first year and realise, despite having radically changed our lifestyle, we were financially no worse off than when we had been living and working in Blenheim. We had taken quite a drop in income over the year but at the same time our outgoings were also down, especially for things like rent and food during those first six months in America and England. With interest rates still high in New Zealand we were having to top up the mortgage repayments on our house and the student house our daughter shared at university. But despite this and ever-increasing bills for things like rates and insurance, we were managing to keep our heads above water. Financially, at least, there was no reason we couldn't go on travelling. Added to that the kids seemed settled, we were greatly reassured about the dog and healthwise we had never been better, with just the odd cold each in the previous 12 months. It was all systems go for another year on the road…

YEAR TWO

○ ○

"If you eliminate smoking and gambling, you will be amazed to find that almost all an Englishman's pleasures can be, and mostly are, shared by his dog."

——George Bernard Shaw

6

As we set out on our second year of travel we hadn't bought a round-the-world ticket as such but instead had stitched together a slightly less adventurous package based on our two main destinations...London and Brisbane. The plan was to fly to Bangkok for a few days on the outward leg and then base ourselves in England for about four months. The deal included a side trip in Europe and we chose Paris, intending to surprise a New Zealand friend who was going to be in France for her 50th birthday. Then, towards the end of October, we would fly south and settle in Australia again, this time in the Queensland capital. The total cost for the two of us including flights, hotels in Sydney, Bangkok and Paris, and with a couple of tours thrown in, was around the equivalent of 2,000 pounds which seemed pretty reasonable.

Saying the last of our goodbyes to our son in Christchurch and leaving New Zealand once more played havoc with our emotions...but our spirits rose appreciably when we were upgraded to business class for the flight to Sydney. Many are called to the boarding gate but few are chosen for the plush seats up front. A gentle, well-manicured hand on my arm, would sir and madam care to come this way? Ah, bliss! So much space! This also partly made up for the fact that we didn't want to go to Sydney in the first place. The itinerary we originally agreed with the travel agent included a direct flight to Thailand but when we went back to collect the tickets we found this had annoyingly been changed. We now had one less day in New Zealand and an unwanted, totally useless night in Sydney. We have been caught in this trap again since, confirming our worst fears that flight timetables and connections between New Zealand and Asia are all now being routed through soulless hotel rooms high above downtown Sydney.

There were further repercussions in this case since nobody had told our Bangkok hotel about the changed flights—we still had the room but when we landed after nine hours in sardine class from Sydney there was no sign of the pre-arranged courtesy pick-up at the airport and we had to fork out for a taxi. Being British we would normally be the ones apologising for all this but just this once we decided to make a fuss. We wrote to the travel agent and Qantas complaining about the way things had been handled and asking what they were going to do about compensation. It's a course of action I can now thoroughly recommend. The travel agent was full of apologies and refunded our taxi fare. Qantas were also sorry to hear how we'd been mucked about and a nice gentleman in Wellington, the director of marketing or some such, wrote back to assure us that if we had any problems in future just let him know.

This document, henceforth known as The Qantas Letter, was squirreled away with passports, vaccination certificates and other important paperwork and produced at various critical moments over the next two years. Like pulling a rabbit out of a hat, the effect was quite magical. Just quoting the letter in a rather injured and belligerent voice enabled us to make occasional but vital changes to flight schedules which common or garden airline staff had previously sworn on their childrens' lives were impossible to alter. After a couple of years this miraculous key to the inner workings of Qantas began to look rather dog-eared. By then I was all for a bit of digital enhancement, changing the date at the top and, hey presto, business as usual, but Maria reckoned, quite rightly I suppose, that we had got our money's worth and should quit while we were ahead.

Our Bangkok hotel seemed identical to every other hotel we saw in the city—a velvety, ornate and cavernous marble and glass mausoleum full of glittering flunkies and an army of discreet polishers and cleaners, invariably glanced just disappearing round corners. We were on the 12th floor, six above the pool and five below the rooftop garden. Though tired when we arrived it was still only about 11pm and around

37C outside, so we decided to go for a quick stroll round the block. It proved an interesting outing. Before long we found ourselves in an area of bars and clubs with topless girls nonchalantly hanging around outside while inside more of the same were distracting punters from their fried rice by attempting to climb up firemen's poles.

As we hovered nervously just inside the door of one bar I experienced my first, and thankfully last, Thai Groin Grab. An old hag lurched off her stool near the entrance and cackling some oriental obscenity snatched my wedding tackle in her gnarled paw and tried to lead me like that towards the bar. At some personal risk I managed to extricate myself, complete a quick U-turn, carve a ruthless path through a fresh throng of eye-popping tourists and tumble out onto the street. Maria, who was unaware of my close encounter with the toothless ancient inside, caught up with me on the pavement. "You okay? You look a bit flushed." Then, her antennae waving jubilantly as she sensed my discomfort, "Bit too much flesh for an old man like you?" "Migraine," I muttered unconvincingly as I lurched off into the neon-lit night.

The next afternoon we took the temples and city tour with an interesting Thai guide who spoke Russian, normally worked with Russian tourists and owned a flat in south London. We visited what seemed like dozens of temples and saw Buddha's of all shapes and sizes from one which was five and a half tons of solid gold to another reclining figure almost 150 feet long. It was all pretty amazing but I thought the traffic we drove through was equally impressive. The streets were jam packed with cars and motorcycles but despite being constantly overtaken by pedestrians, the drivers all remained incredibly calm and good-natured. Whatever other problems they might have in Thailand, road rage wasn't one of them.

A 5.30am alarm call next day signalled the start of what turned out to be 40 hours with virtually no sleep. On another tour bus we spent almost three hours crawling through traffic to reach the outskirts of Bangkok before heading to the famous floating market at Damnoen

Saduak, about 60 miles away. Here we watched in wonder as traders, mostly women, went about their business paddling long, narrow, wooden boats packed with fresh produce, spices and other goods. A few were even cooking on their boats, several of which swayed precariously along with cheerful drivers tending great saucepans of boiling oil. We wandered around buying from some of the boats but drew the line at having our photos taken wearing a live, wriggling and extremely heavy python necklace. However, the tour did cater for exotic tastes and included a display of snake catching followed by lunch at a crocodile farm before we headed off to the Rose Garden. If there are roses here I don't remember them for the main attractions as far as we were concerned were to be found a little way away—a couple of sleepy tigers and loads of elephants.

From time to time you'll read something in the papers about a tourist or two being killed in Thailand at places like this. It's not hard to see how and the only mystery is why it doesn't happen much more often. Those tigers, for example, were in a ridiculously inadequate low-walled enclosure, guarded by a couple of blokes with sticks. The animals looked placid enough but if they suddenly decided to help themselves to some takeaway lunch, watch out! But it was the elephants which posed the greatest danger. People rode them, sat on their knees for photos, even lay down while the huge beasts walked carefully over them. Incredibly, all this was going on in a confined area shared with numerous stallholders and thronging with spectators, a situation so dangerous it simply wouldn't be tolerated by any safety authority in the West. The potential for everything from isolated tragic accident to total mayhem was just mind-boggling.

Our tour included visits to a jewellery factory and a silk and carving centre, and ended with a colourful show featuring Thai dancing and boxing, jugglers and acrobats, plus a parade headed by yet another elephant. Our senses were still reeling from all the sights and sounds and smells of this dazzling kaleidoscopic day when we found ourselves magically transported into another totally different world—inside the belly of a jumbo jet heading for London. The flight was again packed but by now we were sufficiently tired that, after a couple of G&Ts and dinner with wine, we managed a few hours of fitful sleep. We arrived at Heathrow almost exactly a day after waking up in Bangkok. As we banked for our final approach and snatched glimpses of watery green English countryside through the curtain of low, grey cloud, it suddenly all seemed very dreamlike. The stifling heat, the Buddhas and temples and elephants all felt a million miles away from London's crisp early morning June air, the ranks of solid black taxis and a steaming cup of over-priced airport tea. It was good to be back and we were looking forward to seeing what Animal Aunts had in store for us this time.

To find out we actually had to wait another five days. Though we had been in contact with the agency to let them know well in advance when we'd be back and available, they initially had nothing for us which was a little disappointing and disheartening. So, feeling a bit sheepish, we rang friends in London and, despite the short notice, parked ourselves with them for the weekend. On Monday we hired a car and drove to see more friends in Oxford where Maria also had an interview with a nursing agency confusingly called Oxford Aunts. On Tuesday night we were back in London, dining in unaccustomed splendour at the Bombay Brasserie in South Kensington. I hasten to add that this elegant establishment is most assuredly not in the budget bracket and accordingly would not normally pop up in our field of vision. However, an Indian doctor friend whom Maria had worked with in Blenheim suggested the place, met us there and, much to my relief, insisted on paying. It's a magnificent eatery, reportedly patronised by the likes of Prince Charles and some major showbiz celebrities. We knew none of this beforehand so were a tad embarrassed when, expecting an ordinary Indian restaurant, we waltzed in wearing jeans and were politely asked by the maitre d' to check in our small, scruffy backpacks.

The next day we returned to gainful employment with Animal Aunts looking after a rather mixed up mongrel in north London.

George had been rescued by an animal welfare organisation and his owner stayed with us the first day so we could become used to his "little ways". This wonderful euphemism always sets alarm bells ringing and in this case covered a long list of George's personal dislikes—being touched on his hind legs or back, people going near him when he was feeding or sleeping, trying to move him off the sofa, out of his basket or into the car. Breaches of any of those unwritten rules could result in a sharp nip though the doting owner assured us George hadn't actually bitten anyone for, how long was it now, three? four weeks? We were not about to become another notch on George's collar and gave him a wide berth for the two days we were there. I don't know if he really would have gone for us though as we've never yet been bitten by any of the scores of dogs we've looked after. A few have growled and snarled on first meeting but that is usually just nerves and they quickly settle down and accept us. The vast majority, including those proudly referred to by their owners as "superb guard dogs" or "great burglar deterrents", turn out to be great big woolly welcoming mats.

Next up was another short sit in the posh north London suburb of Hampstead where the owners left us with a dog and two cats and could quite easily have come home to no dog and just a single cat. One of the pair somehow crawled into a towel drawer in the kitchen when nobody was around and got shut in. Hours later only one cat turned up to be fed and he was still the only one around at bedtime. So we mounted a search of the four-storey town house and were rewarded in the kitchen with the sound of muffled mewing. Phew!

Our liking for chocolate almost proved the undoing of the dog, a skeletal saluki. We went out for a short walk around the neighbourhood one evening and, without thinking, left a packet of nine little Kitkats on the table. When we came back not only had the Kitkats gone but so had all the wrapping except for a few shreds of silver paper. She was an old dog and we were quite concerned about the effect of a chocolate overdose. Next day we walked her on Hampstead Heath where, like a couple of enthusiastic prospectors working a claim, we sifted her pay dirt hoping to strike if not gold then certainly traces of silver. Though we detected only the merest flecks of silver paper, the saluki seemed none the worse for her binge so we decided to say nothing to the owners. However, afterwards we couldn't help wondering what they must have thought if they noticed their dog's droppings sparkling in the sunlight over the next few days.

Neither of these two sits was particularly memorable but they did tend to highlight the fact that, in our experience at least, really unpleasant Animal Aunt assignments are few and far between. We have had maybe a handful of sits we would really prefer not to go back to simply because both the house and animals were so awful. With the animals that almost always means they are very old, maybe deaf and/or blind, can just about stagger out into the garden and are usually horribly incontinent. Quite often the animals are on some sort of medication and occasionally the owners will tell us up front their pet may not have long to go. Some have even given us instructions about what we should do if the cat or dog does finally slip off the twig while they're away.

But a well-loved pet seems to have an uncanny instinct for survival, going on year after year against all the odds if for no other reason than not wanting to disappoint its owner by dying. One weekend I looked after Sal, a 16-year-old bearded collie belonging to Beverley Cuddy, editor of the popular magazine *Dogs Today*. I think it's fair to say Beverley is more than a little crazy when it comes to all things canine. For example, on the magazine's inside page, where it lists members of the editorial department, I once found Sally, Poppy, Alice, Cleo, Digby, Holly, Daisy, Penny and Molly under the heading "Office dogs". And as if that's not enough, next come Max, Rosie, Misty, Toby and Jet below the banner "Part-time office dogs". Get the picture?

Anyway, in one edition Beverley wrote about the health trials and tribulations Sal had endured and so far survived. The dog had a bad start by contracting the normally deadly parvovirus as a 12-week-old puppy. Beverley said her pet was now deaf and blind and among the serious conditions she had conquered were: a major liver problem, a mammary tumour, a life-threatening infection of the uterus, a stroke, and crippling stiffness in her limbs which meant for a while she had to be carried up and down stairs. Beverley wrote that most recently Sal had needed a general anesthetic to remove a nasty growth on her eyelid and a rotten tooth, on top of which her kidneys had started to go. Beverley acknowledged the end couldn't be far away now, but talk about a fighter…

Touch wood we haven't lost any animals yet—well, apart from a guinea fowl chick which was among a flock of about 20 newly hatched, so that doesn't really count. Our New Zealand friends who introduced us to Animal Aunts were not so lucky. One of their first sits included 12 chickens which, when they forgot to shut them up in the hen house one night, were all killed by a fox. They had to contact the owners in Greece and only then discovered the hens had been virtual family pets, each with its own name. To cover any such accidents, and more importantly calamities like fire, broken Ming vases or the theft of priceless antiques, the agency insists all Aunts join its group insurance scheme. It costs only 20 pounds a year which is a small sum to pay for a lot of sound sleeping.

It was about this time that our travel adventure entered a new phase—we parted company. Nothing personal you understand, purely a financial decision. Maria decided to go off and do a few stints with Oxford Aunts, looking after people, while I carried on with the animals. It was going to mean some short-term separation but on reflection this was probably not altogether a bad thing given that we had been virtually living in each other's pockets for more than a year. The very definite upside was something like another 55 pounds a day coming into the Nelson coffers. And so, for almost the next three weeks, Maria was down near Southampton, several hours south-west of London, and I was well to the north-east in a little village near Ely, in Cambridgeshire. Maria's charge was an affable ex-naval officer known to all and sundry, including his children, as The Captain, while I had my hands full with three cats, two guinea pigs and Albert, a young St Bernard.

Now here's a tip—if you ever see anyone out walking a huge dog, and you feel you have to make a smart comment, try to come up with something original. As an Aunt I've walked such giants as Albert, the St Bernard, Betty, the Pyrenean mountain dog, and Arthur, the Great Dane, and I think I must have heard all the standard quips from other dog walkers and pedestrians, starting with that all-time favourite "Who's taking who for a walk!" Motorists have even been known to make sudden U-turns, slow to a crawl beside us and wind down their windows to deliver such comic gems as "Where's his saddle?", "Hope he's been fed today!" and, yet another example of classic cutting satire, "He's a big dog". People always look so pleased to have thought of something this witty that I try to laugh along while silently groaning on the inside. In the past I've probably voiced my fair share of similarly inane observations which I now fully appreciate are not nearly so amusing the 100th time you hear them.

Albert was not yet three years old and still a very boisterous character who used to pull like a train for the first quarter-mile of his walks before running out of steam. On hot days I used to take him early morning and in the evenings when we'd follow a number of different routes out from the village and across the pancake-flat surrounding fenland. The area was criss-crossed with steep-sided ditches known as dykes which Albert was always eager to try to scramble down for a drink at the bottom. For several days I resisted his charges towards the edge fearing that once down there he would never have the strength to haul himself the almost vertical seven or eight feet back out. I had visions of cows and horses trapped in the depths of these dykes being winched out by tractor...and Albert dragging a Massey-Ferguson down with him.

However, one day he caught me unawares and it was a case of letting him go or ending up in the dyke with him. So I let go. Albert happily paddled, lapped and wallowed and then, to my great relief, used his massive paws with their thick claws to heave himself back up to the path. After that he had free rein to take a dip whenever he wanted and always got out again okay; but there were occasions on these outings when he would run out of puff. Then he would just sink down in the grass like a deflating hot air balloon and refuse to budge for a few minutes until he got his breath back.

As a young and active dog Albert had a prodigious appetite. His daily rations included two very large tins of meat plus biscuits, and as he didn't have a proper bowl the trick was to balance this feast on two dinner plates. The meat and gravy would already be lapping at the edge of the plates when I set them down and as soon as he started hoovering everything up it slopped over in all directions. A fine old mess which Albert would do his best to clean up but despite his efforts the feeding area still needed washing down every day. Afterwards, if I wasn't watching, he would try to dart indoors and tackle the cats' dishes. Not that they probably minded too much as they preferred takeaway food—they were great hunters and I was constantly clearing up feathery remains all round the house.

At this stage we still didn't have a car and at this particular sit I found myself quite isolated. The clients had kindly picked me up at the station when I arrived but there was no car left behind for me. There was not even a village store nearby so when I needed shopping I had to go to Ely on the bus which ran to town and back only once each day. As a result of all this I found I had plenty of time on my hands to walk and groom Albert, feed the cats and clean out the cages of William and Mary, the guinea pigs. I was also spending a lot of time working in the huge and in places wildly overgrown garden. With the warm sunny weather I didn't mind in the least but it was still something of a welcome break when Maria, at the wheel of The Captain's second car, came to visit in the middle weekend.

We made the most of this sudden mobility by exploring the district, visiting country pubs and pottering around Ely. This wonderful little city is dominated by its ancient cathedral, visible for miles around like a mighty ship sailing across the surrounding sea of flat arable farmland. Standing in the quietly echoing coolness of this vast building, which traces its origins back almost 1,000 years, it's impossible not to feel the sheer weight of history hanging in the air. Dotted around nearby are several very old and beautiful monastic buildings; in the chapel of one we were lucky enough to see wall paintings and an incredibly preserved 14th century mosaic tiled floor. And talk about bringing history to life…just around the corner is the house where Oliver Cromwell and his family once lived. And inside the cathedral, attending Even Song in the Lady Chapel, we looked around at statues still headless since Henry VIII's goons went on their Reformation rampage more than 400 years ago.

From the sublime to the ridiculous…it was during Maria's visit that we entered our first world championships. Now normally qualifying for any world champs requires a little expertise, commitment, training or preparation; in this case all we needed was the two-pound entry fee. For this was the world pea-shooting championships which we stumbled upon at some remote village fair as we drove around that Saturday afternoon. For our two pounds we were given slightly wonky plastic pea-shooters and a handful of dried pea ammo and finally called forward with another group of hopefuls to blow, puff, spit and dribble towards the targets. Well, it would be nice to report we were crowned world champs and left with a six-figure cheque, tickets to Acapulco and a lucrative advertising contract with Birdseye. Alas no. Not only were our peas hopelessly off target but we discovered even pea-shooting has its pros…there were guys there with gun-barrel straight metal pea-shooters some of which actually had fitted sights!

Maria was having a fine time with The Captain, nursing him back to health in his beautiful 450-year-old house with its fabulous garden, croquet lawn and sweeping views over the Hampshire countryside. She has done several other Oxford Aunts jobs since and has always found the people incredibly interesting. They tend to be wealthy, older folk and many are able to regale her for hours with intriguing tales of their fascinating lives and the well-known people they rubbed shoulders with. Their houses and surroundings are also usually lovely but being at someone's beck and call almost continually makes the job much more stressful and demanding than looking after animals. In this particular instance she had joined several other staff—two gardeners, a cleaner, a cook and a housekeeper—and complained she was putting on weight with too many rich, regular meals, plus a few tasty snacks in between. Though it wasn't very long since I'd last seen her I thought I detected traces of additional plumpery but naturally was much too diplomatic to say so.

Maria's Oxford Aunts work and the occasional Animal Aunt assignments where we have found a person also in residence, tend to confirm that the well-established aristocracy and plutocracy live in a totally different world. On the whole it's a charming, comfortable, highly civilised and extremely enviable world, but its most defining characteristic is how far removed it is from the day-to-day workings of the planet normal people inhabit. One distinguishing feature of this silver-spoondom is the way in which people cling to old habits and rituals that become part of the fabric of their everyday lives. Their leisurely, golden days, unfettered by constraints of time or money, are studded with little eccentricities which may date back centuries, or at least to the days of nanny and the nursery. Mealtimes provide classic examples. The buying and preparation of food, the exact time for each meal, setting the table, what china and cutlery to use, with similar strict rituals surrounding even such "casual" events as afternoon tea and pre-dinner drinks.

On one occasion I was looking after two dogs belonging to a titled lady from one of the most famous families in Britain. However, when I arrived I was surprised to find I was also looking after her ninety-something-year-old father who was recovering from a recent spell in hospital where he had been given a new pacemaker. Though obviously still feeling a bit weak and frail, he always appeared each morning immaculately groomed and neatly dressed in jacket and tie. I soon found he was one of the most charming and interesting people I had ever met and we spent many hours talking; well, mostly it was him doing the talking with me avidly listening. Among a host of amazing stories he told was one concerning his most recent birthday when family had gathered to celebrate the milestone at a fashionable London restaurant and he had made a speech. The subject, he said, was how he had never made a bed in his life.

As a child he had not needed to make his bed because the family had a nanny to do that. Next he attended public school, where again it was someone else's job to make beds, and then Cambridge University where he and about 50 other students shared a "bedder". He left university in the 1920s and went to work in New York where he was able to afford superior lodgings which included having his bed made. He later sailed to South Africa where, besides rubbing shoulders with such movers and shakers as the Oppenheimers, he and his wife naturally had servants who took care of the bed-making. I'm sure it would have been an eloquent, lively and amusing speech as the old boy had a penchant for telling wry stories against himself. It also served to illustrate the way in which such people live totally different lives to the rest of us. But perhaps the oddest thing is that this well-heeled elite appear genuinely surprised to find everyone else isn't tapping on the shell of a lightly boiled quail's egg at 8.16 each morning, having their hair done at a little place off Bond Street before lunching at Harrod's, bidding a year's wages for a Picasso sketch at Sotheby's in the afternoon, and slurping a stiff G&T by 6.03pm. It is life, Jeeves, but not as we know it…

By now Maria and I were looking forward to our short break in La Belle France but with a few days to fill in first I headed back to London to look after a little dog belonging to a Miss Constance Pettigrew. Now with a name like that I was sure she must be a spinster of advanced years, perhaps an ancient dowager with iron grey hair pulled severely back from a hawk-like face and wearing long black skirts which swept the floor as she walked. Talking to her on the phone confirmed the Dickensian image as she sounded croaky and had a strange accent I couldn't quite place. So it was quite a surprise when I turned up at 7am on the first day and discovered Miss Pettigrew was a ravishing Canadian computer consultant who must have been all of 25. "Call me Connie," she rasped. "Sorry about the voice. I'm just getting over this terrible laryngitis." She had a black skirt too but it stopped well short of the floor. Indeed, that first morning she was ironing it while dressed rather fetchingly in just her blouse and a pair of briefs.

Now, as even my best friends will tell you, I'm never likely to be mistaken for Brad Pitt, so this coquettish display was certainly not for my benefit. It was more likely intended to attract either of two handsome hunks who shared the flat, one French, one Danish, both six-figure bonus boys from the heady world of merchant banking. I felt I had accidentally blundered onto the set of *Friends*. These guys didn't bother much with cooking, cleaning or other domestic trivia. The apartment was a mess but a tasteful, upmarket sort of yuppie mess—partly drunk bottles of water, bits of several different pizzas still in their delivery boxes, empty wine bottles, filters full of expensive coffee grounds and everywhere ashtrays overflowing with half-smoked cigarettes.

This flat was a microcosm of the consumer society run wild. There were designer clothes scattered everywhere…thrown on beds, draped on chairs, dropped on floors, clean and dirty all together, Armani jumbled with Boss mixed up with Gucci and Versace. And money. Literally piles of it. Half a dozen different currencies lying casually around in crumbling heaps of coins and notes, abandoned where it was unloaded from pockets and purses. In amongst all this flotsam and jetsam were such minor items as passports, chequebooks, credit cards and airline tickets. I soon realised these three jumped on planes to Europe and America the way most people jump on a No 48 bus. What they didn't do very often was see each other at the flat; in fact they probably saw more of each other in airport lounges. The second day I was there one of the bankers came in from New York, immediately picked up the ringing phone and went straight out again, back to Heathrow airport to catch the next plane...to New York.

And in the middle of all this chaos was Saja, the sweetest little puppy you ever saw. She was a shiba inu, an ancient breed of small Japanese dog, and was only three months old. She didn't need to go outside the flat and I was just there to play with her, feed her, try to make sure she peed and plopped on the newspaper in the kitchen, and clean up after her when she didn't. Saja was a fluffy brown bundle of mischief who loved to race around the flat, play hiding and stalking games behind the furniture, and have her warm, pink tummy tickled. And like all little pups this age she was a dynamo one minute and flat out asleep the next. Sometimes while hiding behind the couch I would realise it had suddenly gone strangely quiet and creeping out I would find my fierce and fearless pursuer sound asleep on the carpet round the other side. It was a comfortable flat on the top floor of one of those gracious old terrace houses in South Kensington and I whiled away a happy few days there playing with Saja, reading and listening to a CD collection which would rival the stock in most music stores. Oh yes, and waiting in vain for Miss Pettigrew to do some more ironing.

7

Naturally a great many things had changed in the almost 20 years since we lived in England and one of the most noticeable was the way in which the UK was now so closely bound with Europe. The physical manifestation of this was the Channel tunnel linking English and French capitals by a four-hour train ride between the buffers at London's Waterloo and those at the Gare du Nord, in Paris. Attitudes had changed too and people had come to regard the Continent as much more accessible: it was no longer a big deal to pop across the Channel whether for a holiday or just to stock up on duty-free fags. Besides the flow of people, Europe had become one great marketplace with the result that it was almost as easy to buy Continental food in your local Sainsbury's or Tesco supermarket as it was in the shops of Berlin or Barcelona. When we first arrived in England we were struck by the variety of European food on offer particularly after being in New Zealand where, while the food is wonderful, shoppers don't enjoy nearly the choice they have in Europe or the States. At one of our first animal sits we were delighted to find in the kitchen cupboard museli from Spain, berry jam from Sweden, coffee from Belgium, Dutch butter and yoghurt, Italian pasta sauce of course, some Swiss biscuits and a variety of soups from France.

Entering into the spirit of this new-found Continental mobility, we set off at the end of July for a two-and-a-half-day break in Paris. Though we had been there briefly many years before we were immediately overwhelmed by this enchanting city. Arriving about midday on a Sunday, we checked into our hotel and then went straight out sightseeing, walking for miles in the hot sunshine just marvelling at the sheer beauty of the buildings, the bridges, the river, the people. The next day we woke early and headed across Paris to surprise our dear friend Caroline who was just waking up to her 50th birthday. Outside her hotel we had arranged to meet two other good friends from Blenheim who had been holidaying in Finland, and all four of us hid in the foyer with balloons, a birthday banner and, naturally, a bottle of French champagne. On some pretext the hotel manager called Caroline down from her room and she was suitably gobsmacked as we whisked her off for breakfast at a nearby cafe.

We split up afterwards to do our own thing during the day—in our case a wonderful boat cruise down the Seine followed by an energetic climb up the Eiffel tower—before meeting again later for a meal at a Greek restaurant in the Latin Quarter. A memorable evening ended with Caroline and Maria dancing on the tables while I contented myself by enthusiastically smashing all the crockery I could get my hands on before everything on our table was whisked out of reach by anxious waiters. After dinner we took the long route back to our respective hotels, soaking up the magic of Paris by night as we wandered beside the river and across its fairytale illuminated bridges. Next morning the heat, tiredness and perhaps too much vin were taking their toll so we opted for a lazy day browsing around the superb exhibits in the Musee d'Orsay, lingering over a late riverside lunch and scribbling a few postcards before catching our evening flight back to London.

Within 24 hours we were again confronting another of those stark contrasts constantly being thrown up by our travels—this time between Paris and Dartford, Kent, the site of our next animal sitting assignment. Dartford is a drab, depressing, down-at-heel town inhabited by stubbly, tattooed men who dress up in string vests to take their obscene stomachs shopping while their flinty-faced partners scream into pushchairs full of shopping bags and bawling kids. No wonder everyone looked so angry and aggressive; I'm sure I would too if I had to live in Dartford. Luckily this sit was only for a couple of weeks though I think I could have put up with Dartford even longer on account of Max, the Rhodesian ridgeback. Now these large dogs are supposed to be fearless lion hunters from the African veldt but Max was just a lovable, soppy, great big baby. Forget the lions…any yapping bundle of lap dog we met on our walks would send Max into undignified retreat.

He belonged to a lovely young family who'd had him since he was a pup. They told us the tale about how when he was little he used to do smelly farts. At their chorus of "Phew! Max!" and he would stand up and skulk off to his basket in embarrassment. Just for fun they showed us how even today, without a trace of doggy niff in the air, someone can still say "Phew! Max!" and off he trots, eyes downcast, looking terribly apologetic and sorry for himself. Not that his flatulence was entirely a thing of the past. They also warned us this over-sized woosy was frightened of thunderstorms. Well, this being summer in England you can guarantee plenty of good storms and sure enough about a week later—by which time lucky Maria had moved on to another job looking after people—along came a real beauty.

It started about two in the morning, an electrical storm with not much rain but plenty of thunder and vivid lightning which boiled on for the next three hours. Poor old Max didn't know where to put himself. He came in my bedroom, tried scrambling into bed with me, under the bed and finally into the wardrobe. He then padded round the house trying different rooms and bits of furniture but couldn't settle anywhere more than a few minutes. There was no question of anyone sleeping by now so I got up and went downstairs with him. Leaving the light on to make him feel braver, the pair of us snuggled down on the couch and waited for the storm to pass. All this time the atmosphere had been growing increasingly thick as Max the nervous wreck let fly with a regular barrage of real stinkers. For once "Whew! Max!", while entirely the appropriate response, didn't have any effect. Max craved close human company and wasn't going anywhere. Whew! What a night that was!

By the time Max's family returned, Maria was also about to finish her short stay with an elderly lady in Devon who was recuperating after slipping over and breaking her arm. We now had a gap in our Animal Aunt schedule, partly because we had turned down a couple of jobs but mainly because one sit we had been expecting was cancelled at the last moment. Not that it mattered; with Maria already down in Devon we decided to take a week off "work" and explore Devon and Cornwall. I hired a car in Dartford and drove about four hours to meet Maria in the wonderfully-named village of Bovey Tracey. There, a stone's throw from the boundary of Dartmoor, we stayed at the first, and easily the best, of several bed-and-breakfasts we used during the next few days.

The place was run by a wonderful woman called Doris, a superb cook whose mission in life seemed to be to add six inches to the waistline of every guest. Doris, hospitable, talkative and amusing, was born and bred in the area so was a rich mine of local information. We intended to stay just one night but ended up staying three, and as we were the only guests and Doris enjoyed a chat, we were entertained with delightful tales about the local community and her own family. She had three children, now all grown up, and 15 grandchildren, 10 of them belonging to one daughter. It sounded to us as if this daughter was a chip off the old mother-earth block and was certainly destined to be as busy herself in the bed-and-breakfast game, to say nothing of her family's dozen daily lunches, teas and dinners.

From our base with Doris we spent day one climbing Hay Tor, on Dartmoor, and exploring the quaint little seaside town of Dawlish and nearby Newton Abbot. Later we joined an excellent walking tour in the historic cathedral city of Exeter where our route included what was claimed to be the world's narrowest street. However, we began to have our doubts about that a few days later as we met oncoming traffic in the tiny country lanes of Cornwall. Next day we cruised around a number of other picturesque Devon towns and villages, somehow picking up fruit wines, local cheeses, salmon and toasty-warm freshly baked bread along the way. All this was carried back to Dartmoor and as darkness fell that evening we had an impromptu picnic supper on a bench in the village of Widecombe, venue for a fair immortalised in the *Uncle Tom Cobley* folksong. We said fond farewells to Doris in the morning and drove across Dartmoor, past its infamous prison, to Plymouth and from there took the ferry crossing near the mouth of the River Tamar into Cornwall.

It was high season and we pretty much got swept along in the main tourist stream which meant visiting twee little fishing villages like Polperro where today they catch more American, French and German visitors than cod or mackerel. We also took in Truro, Penzance, St Ives and Newquay but didn't bother with Land's End because it was a miserable, wet and cloudy day so hardly ideal conditions to appreciate the rugged beauty of England's most westerly point. As we drove along we passed a number of mysterious stone formations identified as ancient monuments. We stopped at one called The Hurlers and another known as the Merry Maidens where we scored bonus points for seeing a group of bearded, sandal-wearing, lentil heads rapturously hugging the stones. They do say as 'ow folks is strange in them thar parts…

We pressed on to Bodmin Moor and pulled in at Jamaica Inn to soak up a couple of beers plus some of the atmosphere recalled from the novels of world-renowned local author Daphne du Maurier. That night we stayed at a bed and breakfast in Exford, just over the Somerset border, and were woken early next morning by the sound of Exmoor staghounds baying across the misty valley. A few times on our travels around England we have come across hounds out in the field, sometimes with horses, sometimes just with handlers on foot. There's no doubt hounds and horses provide a wonderful spectacle though one day I suspect we'll look back on fox-hunting with the same disgust we now feel for such ye olde pre-TV fun as bear-baiting and cock-fighting. What is surprising, even compared to when we left England at the end of the '70s, is the way foxes have colonised the increasingly urban landscape. At many of the houses where we have stayed, even in heavily populated areas, it has been common to see foxes ambling nonchalantly around gardens or on the road outside. At one house we looked after in a busy street in west London the owners told us how, despite the presence of three noisy dogs, foxes used to come in the garden just on dark to steal the dogs' bones and make off with any toys the kids had left lying around.

After our jaunt around the south coast it was time to replenish the finances with a solid two-week booking in Barnes where we looked after four sibling collies—and for a couple of days five when their mother also came to stay. Barnes is one of those south London areas which, over the years, has imperceptibly become trendy, fashionable and, therefore, expensive. Tony, the guy who owned the dogs, seemed to revel in the self-appointed role of unconventional scruff, the only "real person" in an area of newly-rich poseurs to whom appearance, status and salary were everything. Accordingly he drove the oldest vehicle in the street—a Range Rover, true, but a very old, battered, rusty, oil-leaking model—gave the weeds free rein in his minuscule front garden and made no attempt to fix the collapsing front gate.

To be fair, it wasn't all bloody-minded bravado on his part. Tony was a serious musician, a former session and band player now working from home writing and recording, so his house contained a lot of very expensive equipment. His perfectly reasonable logic was that if burglars were on the prowl they would try every other house in the neighbourhood—all the smartly kept ones with shiny cars outside—before skinning their knuckles on his drunkenly-angled gate. Just the same, we had to keep the front room blinds down the whole time so as not to tempt Fate or any passing light-fingered crim. We were called in because Tony had to fly to the south of France and spend time on his yacht working on a possible music release with an aspiring young Italian singer and song-writer. As they say, it's a hell of a job but someone has to do it.

Tony was devoted to his dogs and we soon discovered why. They were four very different characters, individually adorable and together absolute dynamite. Tommy the Tongue was the sole male. His real name was just Tommy, of course, but we added the tongue bit because his tongue was too long for his mouth and used to always peep out, giving its owner a permanently comical expression. His sisters were Mary, Alice and Dotty, the last dotty by nature as well as by name. The quartet needed unlimited space to work off their incredible energy and that's just what they had within easy reach at Richmond Park. What an incredible place with its wide open areas, herds of different deer, masses of other wildlife and people everywhere riding horses, walking dogs, running, cycling—just enjoying being in beautiful countryside only a stone's throw from central London. One day, after walking the dogs, we returned on bikes and cycled right round the park, stopping nearby for a liquid lunch at The Roebuck pub on Richmond Hill where we sat outside enjoying breathtaking views across the Thames and water meadows below.

Strangely this was the first time we'd had work close to this magnificent royal park though we have made abundant use of its 2,000-plus acres of open space on several assignments since. We would rattle and creak our way there in the protesting Range Rover, find an area without any deer in sight, and let the dogs loose. They would run and play together, swim in the stream at every opportunity and chase down tennis balls with the sheer speed and dexterity of four furry Agassis. They never seemed to tire and would probably have gone on all day given the chance, though we usually drew the line at a couple of hours of exercise in the morning and again later in the day. The four were generally pretty responsive and obedient but even so a special dog trainer visited once a week to reinforce the need for discipline.

The main problem was every so often the pack mentality would kick in and, awash with adrenalin, they would charge off together completely ignoring our whistles, shouts and frantic calling which had people's heads jerking up in alarm 100 yards away. Dear old Dotty was almost always the instigator of these stampedes. She would suddenly stop whatever we were all doing and stare into the distance with her flickering porch light working overtime. She might have glimpsed some far off deer or maybe another dog miles away had caught her attention. Or maybe it was all in her mind. Either way she would suddenly take off. The others, without any idea why, would join in. And that would be that. We'd whistle and shout, they wouldn't stop. So we'd hurry off in their wake expecting any minute to come across a disemboweled deer, a limping labrador or at the very least a well-chewed chihuahua. But we never did and these episodes always ended happily with us meeting the four dogs on their way back with no harm done.

It was during this sit I was briefly diverted to look after two dogs belonging to the previously-mentioned titled lady, along with her charming father, in a magnificent mansion just around the corner from Kensington Palace. The lady herself was already away when I arrived so I was greeted by the Ecuadorian maid who took me to walk the dogs in Kensington Gardens and generally showed me where everything was in the house. We have come across a number of fabulously rich people while working as Animal Aunts but most have either made the money themselves or it has trickled down from their fathers or grandfathers. In this case it was old money, really old money, centuries old money, and it was discreetly there at every turn in the house. The place was huge and beautifully furnished with the most fantastic antiques and paintings, not ostentatiously on display but just scattered casually through each room as part of the everyday decor.

Talk about how the other half lives. You or I might have a fruit bowl in the kitchen with a few apples and oranges in it, possibly some speckled bananas and a couple of dried up mandarins. Here a lovely ceramic bowl you could just about take a bath in was overflowing with 15 varieties of fruit—oranges, apples and bananas plus kiwifruit, avocados, pears, grapes, plums, paw paws, passion fruit, lychees, cherries, nectarines, mangoes and loquats. And these people receive a totally different type of caller at the door. On my first morning I answered a ring at the front door expecting maybe the milkman or postman. Instead I found an immaculately dressed and groomed delivery man from a posh London jewellery shop who was dropping off an equally immaculate package for Lady X.

Early on Sunday morning, August 31, 1997, as I walked the dogs back from Kensington Gardens, I noticed banks of cameras and lights along the pavement near the park. I assumed it was a movie company setting up for a day's filming, not an unusual sight in the capital. However, when I got back to the house Lady X was home and almost in tears at the news that Princess Diana and Dodi Fayed had been killed in a car crash in Paris. Which, of course, explained all the cameras—television and the other media had moved in en masse. Shortly afterwards I went back to the gardens and walked to the gates of Kensington Palace, Diana's official London residence. A steady stream of people, many of them sobbing and looking genuinely shocked, were already making their way through the park to leave flowers at the palace gates. However, this early in the day, before news of the tragedy had fully sunk in, it was still possible to walk right up to the huge ornate iron gates and I took a few photos there of people placing the first flowers. Later, of course, it was impossible to get anywhere near those gates as a vast sea of floral tributes and other gifts carpeted the ground in all directions.

Tony knew he'd be late back from France, probably after midnight, but we agreed to wait even though we were due at our next sit on the isle of Anglesey, in north Wales, the following morning. We had already hired a car and planned to drive through the night, missing all the traffic and catching up on our sleep the next day. So we set off from south London at around 1am and, taking it steady, reached Bangor about five hours later. As we were not due at the sit until 9.30, we curled up in the car on the banks of the Menai Strait and dozed for a couple of hours. Only later did we discover the spot we chose was directly across the water from the house where we were staying. We must have looked a sorry sight when we knocked on the door that morning but despite our bedraggled appearance we were given a wonderfully warm Welsh welcome by the clients and their dogs.

This was one of those blissful assignments where we almost felt we should be paying the people for allowing us to be there looking after their house and animals. The clients were off to Ireland, mixing business with Guinness, and although there were a hundred last-minute things to attend to they made time to walk the dogs with us, explain the workings of their brand new, four-wheel drive Jeep-thingy, and then took us shopping. They lived in a modern, extremely comfortable house built on three levels on the side of a hill with wonderful views back across Menai Strait to the Welsh mainland. Their sailing yacht was moored in the foreground while in the background weary travellers could sometimes be seen napping in cars.

They owned several acres of land nearby which provided ample space to exercise their two elderly dogs, Bosun and Gelert. These labrador brothers, one golden, one black, both slightly rotund and getting on in years, were two of the sweetest dogs we have ever encountered. Our only regret was that, unlike the boisterous collies, these old fellows couldn't manage very long walks; they loved going out but after half an hour or so of gentle rambling and sniffing were beginning to flag. This meant we had plenty of time to ourselves and we used it to explore this part of Anglesey and neighbouring north Wales. We wandered around Menai Bridge, Bangor and the even tinier town of Beaumaris, visited well-known Caernarfon Castle, site of the 1969 investiture of Prince Charles, and drove down to Snowdon, at 3,560 feet the highest peak in England and Wales. When the clients returned we had a spare day which we spent amid the rugged mountains of Snowdonia National Park, hiking towards (but not up!) Snowdon. We stayed one stormy night in the mountains too, at the local youth hostel where, in very severe winter weather, bedraggled long-tailed sheep are said to forsake the meagre shelter of barren stone walls and huddle together instead in the hostel lounge. From our experience that one night I'd say they'd only be marginally warmer inside.

From Snowdonia we faced a long drive diagonally across northern England towards our next sit in Durham. Before leaving Wales we stopped at Conway Castle while back on English soil we couldn't drive through the ancient city of Chester without spending a few hours walking around marvelling at the evidence of history stretching back to Roman times. We drove on through Cheshire, Lancashire and across the Yorkshire Dales and finally to the majestic cathedral city of Durham. As we absorbed England again in this leisurely fashion we became aware of the strangest thing—England was also absorbing us.

For the first time we were noticing things which never registered during all the years we lived here. Perhaps it was because now we had so much more time to see and enjoy whereas in the '70s we were a busy young couple working hard to support two small kids and a mortgage. Perhaps, too, it was because we were exposed only to the fat, prosperous, successful side of England and saw little of the poverty and problems which undoubtedly exist in many areas. And maybe our reactions also reflected the contrast we were experiencing after living in such a young country as New Zealand which was settled by Europeans only 160 years ago. An old or historic building there would hardly rate a second glance in England.

Whatever the reasons, there was no doubt we were seeing England through fresh eyes, appreciating the beauty of the countryside and enjoying the huge amount of history to be found in almost every city, town and village. We were bowled over by wonderfully preserved Roman ruins, churches that had stood for a thousand years or more, streets and buildings which had witnessed slices of history over hundreds and hundreds of years. We avidly studied the blue plaques dotted on buildings around London telling of the famous people who once lived there.

Nor could we quite believe the wonderful walks which criss-cross the English countryside in a network of public footpaths and bridleways. Unlike New Zealand, where farmland is mostly fenced off and inaccessible, here we could wander across fields, walk through woods and legitimately follow tracks running through farmyards and even people's gardens. We were bewitched by vignettes of village life—like cricket matches on the green watched by supporters cradling pints of best bitter outside the ubiquitous nearby pub. Even things about daily life that at first irritated us—for example, village shops and post offices shutting for lunch or closing Wednesday afternoons, or the way some small town libraries close on Mondays—we were coming to regard as rather endearing traits of English eccentricity.

Even much simpler experiences seemed to tap a deep vein of Englishness inside: walking home from the village pub in the dark, picking our way along a country lane to the old gamekeeper's cottage we were looking after, the smell of burning stubble in the air, pressing ourselves into hedgerows at the occasional approach of car headlights. After almost two decades in New Zealand we had convinced ourselves we would never leave; and most definitely we would never leave to come back to England. Now, suddenly, we were not so certain; we found ourselves being drawn back to England which was gradually starting to feel like home again.

Our Durham sit was among the handful we would rather not repeat. It was in a grotty little house where all the furniture was still encased in its original protective plastic covers. A rather strange, sad little man lived there looking after his frail elderly mother. We never saw her as she had been taken into care for several days to give her son a break. She probably needed a break from him too. He was one of those incredibly meticulous and precise people who drive you barmy inside 10 minutes. We spent considerably longer than that going through interminable lists of things like which saucepan to use, where to cross the road with the dog, and how to take the key out of the lock at night and then insert some tissue paper so the cold night air couldn't come through the keyhole. There simply is not enough space to list all the procedures that had to be followed before we could have a bath or bring the car inside the driveway. Not surprisingly the dog, a border terrier, was a neurotic, nervous little thing. We took her on some lovely long walks but were under strict instructions never to let her off the lead. We were tempted but rationalised that in her place we would run off too and never come back.

None of this really mattered though for it was only a five-day job and we had other reasons for coming all the way up to Durham. The main one was to catch up with Chris Mullin, an old school friend now risen to the mighty ranks of Labour MP for nearby Sunderland South. Chris and I had been firm friends at boarding school for seven formative years from the age of 11. We'd spent a couple of summer holidays working together, including a season at a Pontin's holiday camp, travelled around Scandinavia with another friend in an old Bedford van and hitch-hiked down to Rome one summer. Though we went to different universities we still kept in touch for a while but for the last 25-odd years our friendship had been reduced to the exchange of Christmas cards. Despite that I'd followed his public career as an MP and successful writer, and it was great to catch up again. It was also lovely to meet his charming wife and two beautiful little girls, all of whom had until then been just extra names added to his cards over the years. Naturally we took lots of photos together and I take perverse pleasure in noting that maybe—just maybe—he now has less hair than me!

I always find it rather strange how few famous people the people I know know, if you know what I mean. Those who become famous seem to be somehow rationed out among the rest of us so the average peasant can claim to know one or two but seldom more. I think it's fair to count Chris in my quota. Well, he's a Member of Parliament, pops up on television and radio, gets quoted in the papers, had one of his books, *A Very British Coup*, successfully adapted for television, and no doubt kisses his share of babies and cuts miles of opening ribbons.

In fact, when I visited him on another occasion at the House of Commons it was all very impressive—first of all he phoned me from a plane several thousand feet above Nottingham or somewhere to make the arrangements (nice touch that) and then, while we were walking around Westminster, he had to break off for about 10 minutes to do an interview with an American television crew from CBS. Of course he probably spent months arranging that just for my benefit, but still...Incidentally, we were both in the same class at school as Brian

Eno. Brian who? Quite. If we hadn't had neighbouring desks I probably wouldn't have heard of him either. But my as-of-now reclaimed
famous friend Brian has long been at the cutting edge of avant garde
popular music, he's made loads of CDs and recorded with such major-
league stars as David Bowie and Brian Ferry plus bands like U2 and
Roxy Music.

Of course, knowing somebody famous is a great deal easier in New
Zealand. Because the country is more like an overcrowded village it's
almost impossible to pop down to the shops for a pint of milk and the
morning paper without bumping into a film star, a best-selling writer
or a top sports personality, if not all three. Our trump card there is
Anton Oliver. Oh, come on, Anton Oliver, one of the All Blacks rugby
players who went on to captain the New Zealand national team. We've
known him since he was a six-foot, 16-stone nine-year-old (only kid-
ding, but these guys are BIG) when he used to come home with our
son to play after school. If you're from New Zealand, or any of the
world's rugby-playing nations, you'll know the All Blacks are the most
advanced life form on the planet and our closest links to God, and it
really doesn't get much more famous than that.

8

In Durham we had a good look around the cathedral and castle, and once we left the city we carried on in the same vein, cementing our increasingly passionate love affair with all things English. We drove south via Whitby, birthplace of the explorer Captain James Cook who, like us, went to New Zealand though almost exactly 200 years earlier and much less quickly and comfortably. Then to Scarborough, with its magnificent cliff-top castle, and on to York with a stop en route at probably the greatest country house to be found anywhere in Britain, Castle Howard. That night we stayed at the York youth hostel and next day, despite the grey, drizzly skies, we boarded an open-topped bus for a guided tour of the city. We squeezed in a tour of the cathedral and a long rambling walk around the city walls before it was time to leave and head west across the top of England to the Lake District.

I've long since lost count of the number of overseas visitors, particularly Americans, who, when I ask them what they like most about Britain, have immediately answered "the Lake District". Previously I could only admit, eyes downcast with shame, that I had never actually been there in all my 30-odd years living in England. But now, having visited this incredible area, albeit only for a couple of days, I realise what they have all been raving about. It is simply outstanding though I can imagine in the height of summer it must become almost unbearably crowded. We were there in mid-September and even then there were still plenty of visitors around and the youth hostels we stayed at, in Borrowdale and Buttermere, were virtually full.

We came down to breakfast on our first morning to find the place looking like the base camp at Everest. People armed with stout walking sticks and wearing serious all-terrain boots were carrying rucksacks festooned with sleeping bags, tents, little gas cookers, books and maps, water bottles, spare footwear, rolled up rainproof clothing and first-aid kits. The chat, between mouthfuls of hearty English breakfast, was all about where people were going that day and the route they had worked out to take them there; as ramblers good-naturedly shared stories and experiences there was plenty of last-minute adjustment to their day's plans. We, of course, had no special clothes or footwear though we had been studying a map on the dining room wall and decided upon a route for the day. Wearing our usual jeans and sneakers already clearly identified us as raw novices and we were assured rather scornfully that the walk which looked a fair way on the map would take no more than a couple of hours. In fact it took us seven wonderful hours on the most gorgeous of early autumn days.

What those other serious walkers had failed to understand was that the Nelsons, once having girded their loins in the Great Outdoors, place a very high priority on pubs, cafes and tea-rooms, all of which seem to pop up at regular and very welcome intervals in the Lake District. Consequently we were hardly out of sight of the hostel when we came upon the quaintest little tea-room at a place called Watendlath. Sitting outside in the warm morning sunshine with cups of Earl Grey we could just make out some of our fellow breakfasters in their brightly coloured anoraks and thermals crawling like little blue, red, green, purple and yellow ants up the sides of distant hills. And that's pretty much how our day passed—a bit of walking, coffee and homemade flapjacks; more walking, chicken and vegetable pie, coffee and homemade gooseberry tart; some more walking, tea and scones with jam and cream; and finally a little more walking before it was time to sit with a pint of cool bitter soaking up the views of hills and dales, woods, lakes, stone walls and babbling brooks. I mean you've got to have a rest after being out all day in the fresh air walking in the Lake District.

No wonder the two of us were starting to look like a pair of Vietnamese pot-bellied pigs in search of a health farm. It didn't get any better over the next few days as we meandered back down England towards London, staying with various friends and relatives along the way. A couple of days we had breakfast, lunch and dinner with three different sets of people in three different places. At each stop we'd be treated to huge meals and end up eating and drinking far too much and staying up far too late. Extremely pleasant for sure but not particularly healthy. And worse was to come—we were about to head off to Ireland for a week.

They used to be called airline stewards and stewardesses but with everything these days being carefully strained through a fine filter of political correctness they are probably now just plain cabin persons. And plain not just in name: the same process that sanitised the job titles has also ensured that cabin staff are as podgy, pimply, puffy and pasty-faced as their passengers. Indeed, often the only way to tell cabin crew and customers apart is that the crew are the ones who spend most of the time sitting down eating. This policy of the bland leading the bland seems to apply on most western airlines; other national carriers, most notably in Asia, South America and some Arab countries, continue to persevere with the old-fashioned notion that customers prefer to be served by attractive men and women. Given the quality of service on aircraft is now generally way below what you'd expect in your local supermarket, it's probably all academic these days anyway. However, I still think I'd rather my request for another orange juice or a magazine was ignored by a sloe-eyed Singaporean supermodel than by a hairy-lipped British Airways battleaxe wearing a blue serge sack.

Which is why the flight to Ireland was such a pleasant surprise. It wasn't that the cabin crew were all stunningly gorgeous but they did display charm, wit and ready smiles; and they also seemed to have borrowed something from the choreography and costumes featured in the spectacular Irish prancing shows *Lord of the Dance* and *Riverdance*. As we flew out of Stanstead airport on Ryanair's no-frills shuttle service, two of the female crew were animatedly putting together a creative little performance as they took passengers through the routine safety procedures. When it came to demonstrating the lifejackets they tied them so jauntily to one side I half expected the pair to break into a high-stepping tap dance routine and whip aside the dividing curtain to reveal first officer Michael Flatley in all his bare-chested glory.

Of course when it comes to aircraft safety you can rely on the Americans to go several steps further than anyone else in the curious practice of passenger-participation. On some American airlines, depending where you're sitting, you may find yourself with a job you previously thought only trained airline personnel or Hollywood actors were equipped to handle. The safety information card on America West Airlines spells out in great detail the selection criteria for passengers sitting in the exit seats—and their duties in the event of an emergency. These could include assessing whether opening the emergency exit would increase hazards for other passengers, operating the emergency exit, assessing condition of the escape slide, activating and stabilising the slide, assisting other passengers off the slide and selecting a safe path for them away from the aircraft.

According to the criteria, you must be able to hear, read and understand English to fill this role, be aged at least 15 and not be accompanying small children. On our flight one of the exit seats just ahead of us was occupied by an elderly Chinese gentleman who, while certainly meeting the age and childless conditions, obviously didn't speak or understand English. We watched our potential life-saver having considerable trouble ordering tea and later trying to grapple with the concept of either fish or beef for the main meal. We could only guess at his skills in assessing safety conditions outside a crashed aircraft and then conveying his judgement on the smoke, fire and debris hazards to a planeload of panic-stricken passengers. Luckily we never had the opportunity to find out how he might have performed.

Our trip to Ireland was a little bit of returning to her roots for Maria. Her parents were both Irish and when she was a little girl she used to be taken to the Emerald Isle for summer holidays. When I say her parents were Irish I should clarify this by saying they were in fact second cousins and had to get a special chitty from the Pope before they could marry, so yes, very Irish indeed. The area we were heading for was around Westport, on the West Coast, but we first spent a day sightseeing around Dublin. What a city of contrasts. Trinity College housing the 1,200-year-old illuminated Book of Kells, and bullet holes in the Parliament building from the days of the Easter Uprising in 1916; a literary heritage boasting figures like Oscar Wilde, Jonathan Swift, W.B.Yeats and, of course, James Joyce, whose masterpiece *Ulysses* was set in the city; there's 13th century Dublin castle and the much more recent but equally well patronised Guinness factory; and at every turn either a church or a pub.

What we didn't know in advance was that the weekend we arrived coincided with just about the most popular sporting event of the year, the All-Ireland Gaelic Football final. The finalists in this fast, very physical, 15-a-side game were Mayo and Kerry, and as we drove out of Dublin and across to the west coast we must have met practically every supporter coming the other way. Vehicles packed to overflowing with excited fans, flags and scarves flying from the windows, radio aerials and roof, horns blaring and lights flashing, came barreling towards us mile after mile. It was not a good day to be on the roads, particularly not for the three dead dogs and five squashed cats we counted. Each town and village we passed through was trying to outdo the next in its support for one or other of the finalists with banners strung across the road, flags, colourful signs of encouragement and even a few huge effigies of key players propped up by the roadside.

We stopped for lunch at a village pub which, like in one of those science fiction movies where aliens have taken over, was strangely deserted. The place appeared to be run by a handful of children, one of whom went off to find an adult but never returned. These kids had set up a stall outside the pub selling straw hats which they had enterprisingly painted in the colours of the two teams. The oldest, who would have been about 11, was impressing the others by smoking and taking macho swigs from a glass of lemonade. We asked which team he supported and he proudly proclaimed himself a Mayo man. When we asked him why his bravado instantly evaporated to be replaced by a look combining suspicion, alarm and fright that he had somehow been caught out by some clever English trickery. "Don't know" was the best he could manage as he hurried away for a lemonade refill.

The next day on the west coast we saw a pub inviting those who couldn't buy tickets for the game to come inside and watch it on the big screen. "Every time Mayo scores a goal a FREE pint will be given to all the customers," read a sign outside. There were also free half-time snacks, "So come on and join us to watch Mayo beat Kerry." Unfortunately their optimism was misplaced: Mayo should have won but squandered numerous chances and ended up the losers by 13 points to seven. Doubtless the free drinks were even more appreciated in the circumstances.

We stayed at a lovely bed and breakfast between Westport and Castlebar—a place where the unflappable owners didn't bat an eyelid at one family's request for breakfast at two-thirty in the afternoon—and immediately began our search for Maria's distant relations and friends who she'd known only briefly around 40 years before. We didn't really hold out much hope of finding any connections still in the area so it was pretty weird to discover her old childhood playmates were still there. In fact, two of them—a brother and sister, both now married and with kids of their own—were still living within a stone's throw of where they themselves grew up and once spent summers playing with the little girl who came from England for her holidays. Even more strange, when the woman opened her door she knew who Maria was, welcomed her like a long-lost sister and was soon recounting minute details of their childhood adventures which Maria had long forgotten.

Next day we returned for another two hours of reminiscing, meeting her children, and poring over photos old and new. Then it was off in the vain hope of tracking down a distant cousin with nothing to go on except a name from almost half a century ago and a rough idea of the locality. Once again the task proved unexpectedly easy, helped by the fact that, in this part of Ireland at least, people don't seem to move far from where they're born. That plus an almost instinctive Neighbourhood Watch system running through these tight-knit rural communities which means everyone knows everything about everybody. This time we were sorry to find the woman had died 12 months previously. However, Maria was able to have a cup of tea and a chat with her daughter who filled in a few more missing pieces of the family history.

We now set off down the west coast to take in the famed Ring of Kerry and intending to complete our circular tour by sweeping across the south of the country and back up to Dublin. Our route initially took us through Galway and along some rugged coastline where we stopped late one evening to admire, through the gathering gloom and wild sea spray, the towering 650-foot Cliffs of Moher. We stayed the night in County Clare at a budget hostel in Ennis—no towels, no breakfast, not much sleep—and next day drove on through a lush Irish landscape sprinkled with the ruins of churches and castles. We drove to Limerick and Tralee, past piles of peat cut and stacked beside the road, and on to the Ring of Kerry. The countryside, the little towns we came to and the people we met were all so lovely it wasn't long before we were regretting having spent time in Dublin when we could have had a couple of extra days exploring this real Ireland.

As it turned out we were denied the Ring of Kerry's scenic glories by almost constant mist and low cloud. Which might have been just as well as we needed all our concentration just to stay on the narrow, bumpy roads. Although there's plenty of EU money pouring into Ireland these days, precious little seems earmarked for roading projects. The grading and condition of Irish roads completely mystified us and seemed to bear no relation to what was on our maps or, indeed, on the road signs we passed. What on paper appeared as a brightly coloured, dead straight major road would turn out to be a wandering track barely wide enough for two cars to pass. And the narrowest of these roads seemed to attract the most unexpected traffic: women wheeling pushchairs along miles from anywhere, and old men idly poking in hedgerows or standing in the middle of the road intently studying abandoned, rusting pieces of old farm machinery.

We stayed one night in a friendly bed and breakfast high on a hill overlooking Cork and ate a gargantuan Irish breakfast in the morning. Folding ourselves back into the car with some difficulty, we began ticking off an alliterative itinerary of pretty little places—Waterford, Wexford and Wicklow—before reaching Dun Laoghaire where we watched the sun set as we ate fish and chips down by the sea. It was windy but still surprisingly mild considering it was by now October 1. We found another cheap hostel that night and had an early start next day as we had to return the hire car and get ourselves to Dublin airport by 9.45am. Once more we were quickly transported from one world to another—from the peace and quiet of rural Ireland to the hustle and bustle of England where we had to make our way on two airport buses from Stanstead to Gatwick via Heathrow and from there to our final animal sit near Crawley.

When we came to study our moth-eaten bank account it became apparent that for the past few weeks we had tended to do rather more tripping about and sightseeing than working. Our three and four-page long credit card statements filtering back from New Zealand told the same profligate story. However, a much-needed financial band-aid was at hand—I had sold my collection of old postcards. Postcard collecting is a relatively new field compared to, say, collecting stamps or coins. But over the past 30-odd years many thousands of people have taken up the hobby, there are specialised postcard dealers, auctions and fairs, several postcard catalogues and regular magazines and newsletters. The postcards I'm talking about mostly date from around 1900 to 1920. As with stamps and coins there are literally millions of different sorts but only certain ones or types have much value. Common or garden varieties can be picked up for a few pence; the very best ones can fetch hundreds of pounds.

I started collecting before we left England but my interest had waned in recent years and I quite often went many months without buying a single card. That, as much as financial necessity, prompted me to bring the cards with me on this trip and put them into one of the best-known postcard auctions held regularly at Cirencester, in Gloucestershire. Over the years I must have had several thousand cards but by this time I had thinned the collection down to fewer than 500 good quality cards which went under the hammer on September 1. Most were real photographs taken in little towns and villages almost 100 years ago, snapshots of life in late Victorian and Edwardian England. I also had a few cards in various sought-after categories such as railways, ships, certain popular artists, advertising, comic and art nouveau. I love attending auctions but, as I found out this day, the thrill is magnified tenfold when you're the seller. Auctioneer Ken Lawson fairly whistled through the sale but by the end my cards had fetched almost 4,000 pounds with one alone, a photograph of the doomed passenger liner Titanic in Southampton, making 90 pounds. Even after the inevitable deduction of commission and other expenses, this represented a timely transfusion into our anaemic personal economy.

From postcards to green cards...by now we had also taken our first tottering steps along the road allowing us to live and work permanently in the United States. It was a road tangled with red tape and bureaucratic pettiness but we carefully picked our way through it and fulfilled all the requirements however silly some of them seemed at the time. As a result, eight months, three national police checks, one medical, an interview and several hundred pounds later, we were granted our green cards. Of course the American bureaucracy had the last laugh; somebody put the wrong zip code on the envelope, the cards sent to us in Colorado went to the wrong address and then became hopelessly lost in the system. We had been living in the States 11 months and had returned to England again before the cards (which naturally are not green at all) finally caught up with us.

When people ask how we managed to lay hands on the precious and elusive green cards we tell them quite simply we won them in the lottery. We're not being funny…that's what really happened. Every year, as we understand it, the US gives away about 55,000 green cards. It appears these are part of a worldwide immigration quota which is not always fully subscribed because some countries don't take up their complete allocation. If you were born in any of those countries, then you and your spouse are eligible to apply for one of those cards in a lottery system which is advertised in major newspapers around the world. On the strength of my birthplace being Germany we put our names in the hat and, hey presto, the computer picked out Maria Melson, an electronic slip of the pen we soon corrected. One of the conditions involves obtaining police background checks from all countries where you have lived for six months or more. In our case that meant England, New Zealand and Australia, so we started the ball rolling now by sending off the necessary forms for our UK police clearance…the rest would have to wait until we were back in the southern hemisphere.

For our final fortnight in England we again split up though by good fortune we found ourselves only about eight miles apart in Sussex—me looking after animals in Turner's Hill and Maria caring for a very sweet lady in the lovely old village of Rusper. At this sit I had two dogs plus a handful of bantams and chickens; there was also a pet rat and a gerbil but a 17-year-old son looked after them. It was one of those Animal Aunt surprises to find Nicolas in residence, not that it made much difference to me. Soon after the rest of the family left for Florida his girlfriend moved in while an uncle divided his time between the house and his fiancée's place, so it was hopeless trying to keep track of who was coming and going. I had the use of a zippy little Honda so agreed to give Nicolas a lift every morning to the dental laboratory where he worked. I had to get up early anyway to let the chickens out and give the dogs their cornflakes.

I was looking after a large house and garden situated in about 15 acres of meadows and woods. There were plenty of great dog walks from the estate but I also used to pop the pair in the car and take them further afield on other footpaths and to a nearby forest. Maria had three hours off each day so we developed a routine whereby I would drive over to Rusper most days, have lunch with her—usually in the Star, a 500-year-old village pub—after which we'd take the dogs for a walk together. Some of the West Sussex footpaths and bridleways around Rusper are the best we have come across anywhere in England. The two dogs were pretty good though one had a tendency towards selective deafness and once she got a certain distance away, especially if on the scent of something, she would ignore all calls and whistles and just keep going. She was also on a diet.

Dieting dogs are one of the occupational hazards for Animal Aunts. We have come across quite a few and invariably they are real characters each in their own way desperately trying to circumvent the terribly harsh regime imposed by their cruel owners. One porky little Norwich terrier, his rations cut dramatically, was always starving but was allowed a little tidbit for bringing in the newspaper and the mail. It must have seemed quite logical to him that people were greatly appreciative for any kind of paper and were prepared to pay good dog biscuits for it. Accordingly, in his frantic search for additional rewards, he would regularly gather scraps of paper from around the house and present them with such a heart-melting, hopeful expression.

Then there was the cunning old black lab, several kilos over her ideal weight, who would wait until dark before suddenly begging desperately to be let out for a pee. Once outside she would slink away into the darkness as far as the apple tree where she would lay down and, if undisturbed, gorge on the day's windfalls. Another little crossbred terrier we looked after had once been rewarded for jumping up on benches, tree stumps or similar places. Now on a diet, she would still hopefully run ahead through Chiswick Park, in west London, leaping up on every bench, no doubt mystified why her cleverness was no longer being acknowledged. But our all-time favourite was a sweet, dumpy little Jack Russell called Bandit who slept in the same room as his bulk supply of diet food and, you've guessed it, never seemed to lose any weight! Sure enough we soon realised he'd decided to self-administer his diet, burrowing into his dried food sack after lights out and helping himself to generous late night snacks. His owners then invested in a sturdy plastic container with a lid. The next time we visited we noticed Bandit looked considerably slimmer though there was a glint in his bright little eye which suggested he was working on that lid!

We left England for Brisbane on October 23, the very day after we had woken to find everything outside covered in the first frost of winter. How lovely to be leaving all that behind and heading into another summer. However, the flight down to Australia was another matter. We flew out about 10.30pm after a long day but the plane was so packed sleep was out of the question. It also didn't help that we ate and drank too much initially and by the end of around 25 hours of travel we were like a couple of zombies. The plane touched down in Bangkok where we felt a bit better for stretching our legs in the airport. We managed to snatch a bit of sleep on the next leg to Sydney and as we flew over Western Australia we could look down five or six miles and see widespread bush fires burning in the darkness. After Sydney the plane was, ironically, almost empty but of course by then we only had about an hour to enjoy the space. We arrived in Brisbane at 8.15am local time feeling distinctly odd and it was a good 24 hours before all the bits of our bodies seemed to catch up.

It was really a mistake to do such a long trip in one go and we promised ourselves then that in future we would always have at least one stopover, maybe a couple if we had the time and money. Put it down to short-term memory loss but a little over 15 months later we're flying from London down to New Zealand and what happens? Not only do we make the trip in a single, interminably long, nightmarish journey but this time we're not even flying in the relative comfort of a British Airways or Qantas jumbo—we're on a cheap Britannia charter. This really was the flight from hell.

We were in a middle row of four seats with Maria crammed next to two of the fattest, most revolting creatures imaginable. In any other situation we would have moved as far away as possible from these hideous cretins but on a crowded plane there is no escape. The pair of them coughed over us the whole way as did the bloke sitting right behind. The man sitting half in Maria's seat stank of stale booze and cigarettes and had terrible body odour; what made it worse was that he wouldn't keep still and spent the whole flight fidgeting about and getting up and down. Another endearing habit was blowing his nose on paper tissues, minutely examining the results with grunts of evident satisfaction, and then ramming them into the seat pocket in front. I won't attempt to describe how disgusting it was at mealtimes.

The plane touched down for re-fuelling three times—at Abu Dhabi, Indonesia and in Brisbane—before eventually reaching Auckland. Each time we were among the first off, desperate to make the most of an hour or more of relative tranquility. Needless to say, we have now added to our vow about stopovers—we'll never fly long-haul charter again. Indeed, we are seriously thinking of blowing all our frequent flyer points on an upgrade to business class next time we face a long distance flight. The thought of those huge, comfy seats and all that leg room is one reason; the other is the sheer bloody pleasure of knowing just what hell everyone else is going through back there in zoo class.

9

Brisbane had really been Maria's idea and initially I had not been so keen. I had probably enjoyed Melbourne more than her and would have been quite happy to go back there. However, one of our unwritten rules was to keep moving on and trying new places, so returning to Victoria was really out of the question. I also imagined Brisbane might be too hot and sticky in the summer and I had not been particularly impressed by the city or surrounding area when we had briefly been there on a previous holiday. Not for the first time I soon came to appreciate just how right Maria was and how misguided I had been. Brisbane, our home for the next 11 months, was absolutely brilliant.

What I had failed to fully appreciate on our earlier fleeting visit was what a beautiful city Brisbane is and how the Queensland capital is making full use of its greatest asset—the river. Expo had been staged along the south bank of the river in 1988 leaving behind an infrastructure of buildings and boardwalks which the city has now added to, updated and improved. On one side of the Brisbane River lies the city centre, fronted by a handful of the most stunning high-rise buildings we've seen anywhere, and nearby the lush and bountiful Botanic Gardens. On the opposite side, the south bank is dotted with restaurants, markets and other entertainment, while not far away are the cultural bits—the State library, art gallery, museum and performing arts complex.

Further along the same side, linked by the boardwalk, cycleways and walking tracks, are well-used picnic areas, a man-made lagoon with sandy beaches, and a cliff face which constantly challenges climbers, day and night. All these attractions, immaculately maintained, naturally had the effect of bringing huge numbers of people to the riverside.

But it was always a surprise to see how many came after dark—to climb, cycle, walk, barbecue their evening meal and swim—especially in the warm summer evenings when they emerged from the concrete jungle to cool off and have fun alongside this human watering hole.

So much for what's beside the river...what's on it is just as exciting. There have long been paddle steamers and various cruise boats, loads of yachts and smaller craft, plus a few water taxis ferrying passengers across the river at busy junctions. Then, just less than a year before we arrived, the city council, in a blinding flash of genius, introduced the CityCats. This fleet of sleek, streamlined, 140-seat catamarans purr effortlessly up and down the river, taking an hour to complete the full trip from Brett's Wharf to the University of Queensland. In between they zig-zag back and forth across the river, picking up and dropping off passengers at around another dozen points. These boats have been such a success that about the time we left they were on the point of introducing a half-sized version, the KittyCats. Sadly these lasted only about 10 months before the authorities decided their wash wasn't environmentally friendly enough for the river's ecology.

In the mornings and evenings the boats are packed with commuters; at weekends they are solid with tourists; the rest of the time they are the preferred means of transport for thousands of people who just love to glide up and down this wide, winding, glassy, classy river. The Cats have to throttle back within the city speed limits but once beyond those boundaries they fairly nip along and people love to stand at the bow, especially in the darkness of a tropical evening, and be gently ruffled by the cooling breeze. Not only do the Cats offer a great ride but the fares are very reasonable, particularly for those buying a special all day Rover pass or commuters with weekly or monthly season tickets. Indeed, it's such a good deal that when the Cats were first introduced families used to happily clamber on board for a day out. According to folklore clandestine picnics on the Cats were a popular practice though most people had the good grace not to bring their own deck chairs. Today the city frowns on such unbridled travel and, depending how busy things are, passengers who complete a two-hour round trip may be politely encouraged to disembark.

We instantly fell in love with all this but Brisbane had plenty more to offer: wall-to-wall sunshine, a balmy semi-tropical climate, scenery which was out of this world, luxuriant plant growth and some surprisingly exotic wildlife. The people we worked with and got to know were as warm and friendly as their climate, with an equally dry sense of humour. Then there was the food, especially the seafood, the fresh fruit and vegetables. Just amazing and maybe even tastier than in New Zealand which until now we had always considered the world's best. And talk about value for money…well, certainly after coming from England it was just plain cheap. Indeed, after stepping back from the brink of an English winter, almost everything about Brisbane seemed like paradise.

These were pretty much our first impressions and, to be honest, they hardly changed the whole time we were there. On our second night we caught a Cat down river to a renowned seafood restaurant at Brett's Wharf. We sat outside with our drinks and black seared marlin watching a group of comical pelicans jostling for space on jetty posts as they settled down for the night. And as the last of the day drained from the sky it was hard to suppress a smile at the thought of people in England about to set off for work but first having to scrape the ice and frost from their windscreens. Normally when you see or do something for the first time there is always a little touch of magic about it which is hard to recapture subsequently. However, in Brisbane we found the magic didn't wash off so easily and continued to cast its spell time, after time, after time. Even three years later, when we called in briefly to re-visit old haunts, Brisbane plucked and teased at our senses just like before and we were struck by how easily we could settle down there again.

As usual, we had arrived in a new country hardly knowing anyone, with nowhere to live and no jobs lined up. On all counts we were destined to be incredibly lucky. We arrived on a Friday, spent the weekend in the youth hostel and by Monday were in our own furnished flat. Looking for accommodation in the paper we had no idea where the various streets or suburbs were. So, completely at random, we picked an area called Kangaroo Point simply because it was close to the river and within easy reach of the city. On the Saturday we found an estate agent there who showed us a couple of places. One was small but with great views, the other much larger but with no views. We went with the views.

We were in an unremarkable square box of a building full of identical one-bedroom flats which were surprisingly cheap at 150 dollars per week given the million-dollar views, 24-hours-a-day, across the river and into the high-rise canyons on the edge of the city. Only the boardwalk and the grounds and swimming pool belonging to the apartment building separated us from the river. From our tiny second floor balcony we could watch the boats coming and going and, with a strong pair of binoculars, probably eyeball several thousand office workers as well. The view, amazing enough by day, became absolutely jaw-dropping after dark. Most of the buildings were lit up all night while on the water party boats and paddle steamers, decked out in strobe lights and fairy lights respectively, glittered up and down the river.

The downside was that the flats were very compact and ideally suited to just one person. There was only one large living area sandwiched between a good-sized bathroom and a balcony. The bed was at one end and at the other was a kitchenette complete with sink, fridge and cooker. A few owners in the block had bought two adjoining units and knocked them together which was really the only practical long-term solution if two or more people wanted to live together without one eventually throttling the other. For quite a while the lack of space didn't bother us. We didn't have much stuff to spread around—everything still fitted into two backpacks—and after 16 months on the road since leaving New Zealand we were well used to living in close quarters with each other.

But despite all that, what Maria lightly called "cabin fever" had begun to set in after a few weeks. In other words, we had begun to get on each other's nerves. This, coupled with the imminent arrival of our son William, meant it was time to find something a little more spacious—three people in that flat would definitely not have worked. And so, five weeks after moving in, we were moving on...and moving up. We found a place on the 12th floor of a hotel and apartment complex only about 150 yards away across the thin neck of land where the river snaked around the tip of Kangaroo Point.

Well before then, however, we had both started work. Maria had done her usual trick of walking into the nearest hospital—literally two minutes from our door—presenting her CV and references, having an interview and being almost begged to start work the next day. What a career nursing is, what a passport to work almost anywhere in the world. Don't put your daughter on the stage Mrs Worthington but do put her in the theatre...the operating theatre. Maria joined the hospital's bank of on-call nurses. In theory that meant intermittent work and being called in to fill gaps when people were sick or went on holiday. In practice it meant there was work virtually every day if she wanted it and sometimes they were so desperate they tried to persuade staff to plough on through 16-hour double shifts.

I had embarked on my familiar search for media work. I walked miles out to the offices of the Brisbane *Courier-Mail* to see what was available and while there I flicked through back issues of the paper's jobs section. I saw an advert for a casual journalist to work in the public relations department at the University of Queensland. Well I'm pretty casual, I thought, so I gave them a ring even though the closing date for the job was well past. They were about to start interviewing but said to send in a letter, CV and clippings which I did next day. I also applied for a couple of other writing and editorial jobs but it was disappointing to see how little was on offer. Meanwhile, not wanting a repeat of the barren weeks of waiting that happened in Melbourne, I turned to something I now knew would at least bring in some steady cash—market research.

Two days after Maria started work I joined a training session with a company called Roy Morgan Research which had offices only a 15-minute walk away from our flat. However, this work was different to what I'd done in Melbourne—instead of pounding pavements and knocking on doors, we just had to sit at desks with a computer screen in front of us and do all the interviewing on the phone. In order to impress at the interview I must confess, in addition to my Melbourne experiences, I invented a couple of fictitious telephone research jobs in England. Of course I realised afterwards I needn't have bothered: these people were pretty desperate too and were hiring everyone who walked through the door with the possible exception of deaf mutes. Woody Allen once observed that 98 percent of life is just turning up, which makes me wonder if he started off in market research.

The very next day I began my regular shifts which were in the evenings between 4pm and 8pm, plus some weekend afternoons. There was no doubt it was easier than tramping door-to-door but conversely it became stale and boring very much more quickly. In fact, by the end of my first four hour shift. Occasionally the surveys were more interesting, such as when we were recruiting people for television talk-show audiences, but mostly it was a cruel test of endurance and sanity.

I couldn't help feeling that ringing people at home in the evenings or weekends was a much greater invasion into their privacy and personal space than knocking on their door. A number obviously agreed and were extremely curt and often very rude as soon as I launched into my introductory remarks. In these circumstances my English accent acted like a red rag to a bull and definitely increased my tally of f****** refusals, to borrow a rude word I came to hear frequently on the other end of the line. However, I was constantly surprised at how polite and cooperative the vast majority of people were. I must admit when I get called by one of these companies at home now I always answer the survey knowing that I'm helping to put a little extra bonus in some poor sod's pay packet.

In the midst of all this came one of the more traumatic moments of my life—I turned 50. As befits such a milestone, or should that be millstone, it was definitely a birthday with a difference. Maria and I took off to Dreamworld, one of the theme parks on Queensland's Gold Coast. Our day there included expending several pints of adrenalin on something called the Tower of Terror, billed as the tallest, fastest and several other "ests" ride in Australia, if not the world. We sampled various other rides and attractions, including a water slide which seemed to fall almost vertically for about two miles, but the highlight of the day, and the main reason for our visit, were the Bengal tigers.

Dreamworld had seven of these magnificent animals—some white, others wearing the more traditional black and orange strip—which spent much of their time outside in a huge enclosure romping, paddling and playing games with their keepers. For periods nothing much might happen, the big cats just walking around, sitting quietly or snoozing while the keepers waited with them, chatting to visitors and answering questions. But when playtime started the physical interaction between tigers and humans was absolutely stunning to watch. Despite the obvious potential danger to the keepers, whenever Dreamworld advertises a vacancy they are flooded with applications from people wanting to do the job, and it's not hard to see why. When we got back to Brisbane that evening there were cards and presents to open, plus faxes and phone calls from friends in New Zealand. And a day which perhaps wasn't that traumatic after all ended directly across the river from our flat in a swish Italian restaurant where I had the most unusual and delicious meal of pasta and fresh Queensland crab.

With Roy Morgan I was earning about 50 dollars for each shift and after a couple of weeks, with nothing more permanent yet looming on the horizon, I added a weekend breakfast cereal survey for another company. This research meant trudging the streets again though the project was unusual since we paid people hard cash for taking part. The rate varied between 10 dollars, for the short version of the survey lasting only a few minutes with people who were not really breakfast eaters, and 30 dollars, for a session that involved quizzing a mother of young children for well over an hour. Once again quotas severely restricted the people we could talk to and the survey quickly became a real slog. After 16 hours that first weekend I had just seven completed interviews, which turned out to be three more than anyone else.

My future prospects were starting to look a little grim when Lady Luck suddenly stepped in. Out of the blue the university called me for an interview on the Monday. Despite the heat, I got all dressed up in my thick woollen English suit and by the time I arrived I was beginning to melt. Nerves sent my temperature soaring another few degrees when I found myself facing a semi-circle of four interviewers—Tony Murray, the boss man, and the three women who ran specific sections within the department. I could feel torrents of sweat cascading down my body and was considering asking for a break, so I could at least wring out my socks and underpants, when the interview was mercifully over. They said they'd let me know on Friday but instead rang on Wednesday and I started work on Thursday. It was almost like being a nurse…

I don't know why, in 25 years as a journalist, I had never before considered working at a university. I have since repeated the exercise in America and, on the strength of those two experiences, can honestly say universities provide the best working environments I have ever found anywhere. To begin with the physical surroundings and facilities are outstanding. Invariably the buildings are a wonderful mixture of old and modern, set in acres of pristine gardens, lawns, trees and fountains, all beautifully kept by an army of gardeners and groundspeople. And inside those buildings are to be found everything from the latest computer labs to the oldest libraries, from scanners of the human body to scanners of the heavenly bodies, to say nothing of the cafes and restaurants, the gyms, pools and sports fields, the theatres and cinemas. Universities are like small, self-contained towns, the main difference being everything in them is generally more affordable, higher quality and better maintained.

Then there are the people who inhabit these places. Anywhere where several thousand young people live and work much of the year has to be a vibrant and exciting place, always buzzing, always bustling, always full of life. A lot of my work involved writing about what was happening at the universities in terms of research and other news-worthy and ground-breaking stories. Which meant, among other things, I was dealing every day with extremely clever people but also people who were incredibly interesting and keen to share their knowl-edge with a wider audience. My experiences in Australia and America must have taken me into just about every university department and exposed me to a vast treasure chest of material which would surely quicken the pulse of any journalist. It certainly fired me up. I could not believe the great stories that just kept coming across my desk day after day.

With a student population of around 28,000, UQ, as it was popu-larly known, was the largest of five universities in Queensland and one of 37 in the whole country. The main campus, a few miles from Bris-bane city centre, fanned out from the sandstone cloisters of the Great Court, bordered on one side by the trendy little village-like suburb of St Lucia, and on the other by the river. Just walking to work through part of the campus every morning was enough to lift my spirits. I would pass the Olympic-size open air swimming pool, a maze of tennis courts, a fantastically appointed gymnasium and the Schonell Theatre, which was not only a cheap place to see movies but was reputed to have the most comfortable seats—more like leather armchairs really—of any theatre in Queensland, if not Australia.

The year I was at the University of Queensland it was voted Austra-lian University of the Year, though to be honest I can't claim all the credit for that. I was appointed initially on a six-week trial basis, work-ing full time but splitting my week between two different sections within the Media and Information Services department. Three days a week I worked for Jan King, head of media liaison, writing stories for local, national and international media, telling the world about the great things going on at UQ. Another significant part of the job was helping newspaper, television and radio journalists with their own stories by putting them in touch with experts from the university's huge bank of talented staff.

The other two days of the week I would physically pack up all my pens, papers and notes, my folders and files, in-trays and out-trays, and move across the hallway into another office with a different desk, computer and telephone. This was "special projects" where we worked on producing *Contact*, a twice-yearly glossy magazine, the university's annual report, the yearly research review, plus a whole miscellany of other publications from departmental handbooks to brochures. Staff in the public relations department, there were around 20 of them, were generally a great bunch but Jan was definitely my all-time favourite. She came with an impressive pedigree in the usually ruthless and cynical world of media and PR yet she had managed to remain a lovely, gentle person besides being an incredibly industrious and conscientious worker.

When I joined the team it took me a while to adjust to a number of radically different ways of doing things. Two of the most fundamental differences between this job and what I was used to as a daily newspaper journalist were the volume of work expected and the speed at which it was required. On the newspaper there was always pressure to produce more copy while at the same time meet tighter and tighter deadlines. At UQ it was suddenly all very relaxed and laid back. The whole system was geared to a comparatively slender output per person and only very rarely was there a deadline looming in under a week.

Something else that took time getting used to was the multi-level checking system which, while an almost foolproof way of eliminating errors, was a time-consuming luxury most daily papers cannot afford. Our copy first went to a central editor who checked it as much for house style as for content and consistency. Next, and this was also pretty much unheard of in newspapers, it was sent back to the original source for checking. As a journalist I had always lived by the creed that quotes were sacrosanct: if something was in quotation marks, then it had to be exactly what the person had said. Now it was suddenly okay to stick quotation marks around virtually any paraphrasing; indeed, there was almost an unwritten rule that we wordsmiths would lighten up, brighten up and generally polish the pedestrian prose of the academics. And since they were given the chance to see the end result and change anything they didn't like, this probably made good sense.

After all corrections had been done, the story finally went to Tony Murray whose antenna were always twitching for anything the least bit politically sensitive or which, however true and accurate, could still rebound to the detriment of the university. His was a thankless task. Whenever he changed our copy we moaned and complained he was being an over-cautious, inflexible pedant. However, when he occasionally dropped his guard and let something controversial go through, he risked getting it in the neck from higher up the chain of command, usually the vice-chancellor. Universities seem to share a common ambivalence towards the media, veering wildly between the sycophantic and the schizophrenic. They employ clippings services to provide daily evidence of their success in placing stories in the press while television and radio coverage is also carefully monitored. Yet senior staff are apparently afflicted by the same genetic disorder which renders them incapable of recalling hundreds of very positive stories while equally unable to forget the handful of less flattering ones.

One of the things I liked best about working at the University of Queensland was I could commute by boat. Living on Kangaroo Point we were already used to taking water taxis across the river to the city or slightly down river to do our supermarket shopping in the suburb of New Farm. It was just such a lovely way to travel and, we fondly imagined, a bit like living in Venice. Now my daily journey began with one of the little water taxis that I could watch from the balcony of our flat as it bobbed across the river towards the landing stage about 50 yards away. On the other side I caught a CityCat all the way up river to the university, a wonderful 30-minute trip. Standing on deck at the back of the catamaran, I could look up at our flat and see Maria waving from the balcony until we rounded a bend and were out of sight. For the first couple of weeks I spent the whole journey standing outside, drinking in the wonderful views and intoxicated by this sensational way of going to work. As time went on I gradually began to retreat out of the hot sun and settle down inside the cabin with a good book. During our 11 months in Brisbane I read 31 books, almost all of them while gliding serenely up and down the river.

At about this time Bob Boyes, the man who was looking after our property in Blenheim, showed up in Brisbane. He was in Australia preparing some contract documents for his company back in New Zealand and rang us out of the blue one day. As luck would have it he was staying in the Dockside Hotel, also on Kangaroo Point, so we popped round to see him and collect some mail he had brought for us. He was staying in a swish double-room spread on the top floor of the hotel and, coming from our tiny flat round the corner, we were immediately envious of how much space he had. Little did we know that three weeks later we would be living in this luxurious hotel building ourselves in an identical apartment just one floor below.

Feeling that the walls of our flat were definitely starting to close in a little bit every day, and with Christmas visits from the kids again looming on the horizon, we had begun looking around for a larger place to live. We saw several flats we liked but kept coming back to the Dockside Hotel. Although it was called a hotel and was a magnificent establishment, comfortably four stars going on five, a number of the units had been sold off privately. The owners lived in some of these but others were rented out through a local estate agent. We were especially impressed by the size of the one-bedroom apartments which dwarfed the space, comfort and facilities we had in our small flat. The two-bedroom, two-bathroom units were positively palatial and we decided, at least for the time both kids were with us, this was what we needed.

After they left we could downsize to a one-bedroom unit...or so we thought.

The cost of these larger units made us pause—they were 340 dollars a week, so hardly in the budget travel category to which we had become accustomed. However, we were now both earning quite good money and we reckoned we could afford to splash out on a little luxury. I was at work the day Maria went round to Dockside with the agent to look at three available units. They were on different levels and faced different directions, and in the end she chose the 12th floor overlooking a small marina. Here we swapped our grandstand seat in front of the city's bright lights for the most wonderful sweeping views down the river towards New Farm. From our balcony we had a birds-eye view of all the river traffic besides looking out to the famed Gabba cricket ground, over rooftops and across the distant Botanic Gardens towards Southbank, and away on the horizon to shimmering hills and bush. We could even see, about half a mile away, the hospital where Maria worked, though this was not her favourite view.

It wasn't long after moving into Dockside we came to appreciate that while we were paying a lot to live there, we were also getting a lot more for our money. First and foremost we were getting air conditioning. It was now December and approaching high summer in semi-tropical Brisbane which meant it was becoming very hot and humid. It was pretty warm by six in the morning and distinctly sticky by seven when I would see people boarding the water taxi with their shirts or blouses already soaked in sweat. Maria and I were amazed to find most people we met and worked with did not have air conditioning and simply relied on electric fans. Since it was often almost as hot and humid at night as in the day we couldn't understand how they ever managed to sleep, and certainly during the worst of the heat spells some colleagues wore permanently exhausted expressions. One guy I worked with was always delighted to come to work and sit in a cool office, and would cheerfully report on spending hours at weekends shopping with his wife or watching naff movies with his sons, so long as it was in air-conditioned buildings.

Our first little flat had air conditioning but it never worked properly and struggled to make much of an impression. Often it was only the incessant drone that indicated it was even switched on; there was no way of telling from the temperature. Walking into Dockside, on the other hand, was like wrapping ourselves in a soft, fragrant mist. The entire building was air-conditioned and the effect was immediate; by the time we had travelled up 12 floors in the lift and reached our apartment, the heat, sweat and dust of the day were a fading memory. Even the cool shower we'd been fantasising about all the way home suddenly seemed unnecessary. Which was saying something in Maria's case as often she'd spend boiling afternoons struggling to manoeuvre senile old girls around hospital wards until she was drenched in sweat and almost as dazed and confused as her patients.

The downside was that having sipped the sweet, chilled nectar of this champagne air we became reluctant to leave the apartment and venture outside again. It was the opposite of living in a cold climate where you slog home through snow and rain and icy winds, become all warm and snuggy once you are inside, and don't want to go out again. Which was another of the great advantages of living in Dockside—the hotel was part of a complex with bars, restaurants, a comedy club, general shop, doctor's clinic, gym, tennis courts and swimming pools all on tap. So even in the hottest weather, we never needed to venture far from our air-conditioned eerie on the 12th floor.

I was loving the work at university and they obviously liked me a bit too because after just two weeks I heard on the grapevine my employment was being extended a further six months. Then, only about a week later, the boss called me in to say my contract was being renewed for a full year. The variety of work was astonishing. Assignments used to come in all the time but as I got to know people and find my way around the campus I began generating more and more of my own stories. There was masses of exciting health and medical research going on

which always got a good run in the media. But since we tried to maintain a system giving publicity to every area of the university, from
anthropology to zoology, we would go out of our way to dig up interesting copy from such seemingly unpromising sources as philosophy,
languages, history, religion and law.

I must admit stories sometimes became pretty technical, especially
from some of the more pointy-headed researchers in the physics or
chemistry departments. Or perhaps it was just that these were my
weakest subjects at school. Either way there were times when I'd return
to the office after an hour's interview, my notebook bursting with
information none of which I really understood. Then there was nothing for it but to cobble something together and hand it in like a reluctant student hoping for at best an E for Effort but more likely an F for
Fuckwit. Except that I had the added security of knowing Professor
Whatshisname would still have the opportunity to knock my meaning-
less drivel into shape and sense further down the track. The scary part
was that occasionally these blundering bluffheaps of mine came back
virtually unchanged.

Early on things didn't always go as planned. Besides getting lost
fairly easily on the campus, one of my major embarrassments was going
on assignments only to find they had been covered very adequately perhaps a year or maybe only a few months earlier. I then had to struggle
to find a new angle but sometimes there really wasn't one and I had to
sheepishly apologise for wasting everyone's time. One of my first jobs
involved interviewing a professor who was based at a psychiatric hospital in Brisbane. He met me at reception and we rode the lift up to his
floor where he showed me around and we did the interview. However,
he had an unusual name, something like Gammeon, which I carefully
spelt back G for George, A for Apple etc to make sure I got it right.
When I reached the final letter and was about to say N for Nuts I suddenly remembered where we were. In a flash my mind went blank and
I couldn't think of a single word beginning with N before lamely coming up with Netherlands.

By this stage I could feel the onset of one of my rare attacks of the giggles, so I hastily concluded the interview, said I could find my way out and headed for the lift. However, somehow I stopped at the third floor instead of ground level, and emerged into an area packed with patients many of whom were holding serious discussions with inanimate objects, closely examining their clothing or pacing anxiously up and down. Spotting a reception desk at the far end of the hall I made my way through the crowd and asked for the way out. A kindly lady explained I was on the wrong level and would have to go back to the lift and down another three floors. As I turned I realised I had gathered quite a crowd of followers. Once more my fit of giggles bubbled up to the surface and trying to keep a straight face I began hastening towards the lift, outpacing several of the anxious pacers along the way. As the lift jolted its way to the ground floor I glanced at the little notice you always find inside about the capacity and servicing and saw the company responsible was Schindler Lifts. The vision of Steven Spielberg turning up to repair the elevator was a bizarre image too far and I finally staggered out of the building with tears rolling down my face.

Many of the stories from UQ were so good they simply sold themselves—we just sent them out and news editors everywhere pounced on them, either running our versions or putting their own writers on the case. Other stories with less obvious appeal either went to more specialist publications or writers, or else needed a few phone calls in advance to whet media appetites.

Certain subjects always went down especially well. Witches and pagan rights were surprisingly popular while famous people, making money and UFOs were other subjects guaranteed a good reception. And anything to do with sex, of course, was an instant best-seller. Which led to an unauthorised, short-lived and very merry competition to see who could weave the most sexual references into their stories. For a while steamy stories began appearing with X-rated descriptions of sexual encounters between everything from turtles to mice to things so small you needed a microscope to see what the hell they were doing.

I scored especially highly with a story on bearded dragons, a type of lizard which is apparently a raving reptilian sex machine. I followed this with another major sex exposé, this time featuring little furry marsupials called antechinus which dedicate their entire existence to sex—the males mate and then die, the females breed and then die. A Danish student was investigating all this mating business for her PhD, surely paving the way for some future tabloid headline to scream: "They're at it all day claims sex-mad Scandinavian blonde bombshell." However, Tony, who seemed to have a finely-developed prudish streak even where amoeba were concerned, sensibly spiked most of our light-hearted efforts to re-invent UQ as a hotbed of sexual intrigue merely masquerading as a place of higher learning.

At the same time as writing a huge variety of copy myself, I was enjoying the novelty of helping other journalists find and write their stories. I had always worked in fairly competitive media environments where, while maintaining friendly relations with rivals, we were careful not to give anything away. When friends from another newspaper or local radio station popped in for a chat, we took care to put away diaries, notebooks or anything else that might give a clue to what we were working on.

Now I found myself expected to cough up all my stories, notes, leads, ideas, anything remotely useful, to any journalist who thought to pick up the phone. Often they wanted specific information or people to talk to, but sometimes they were just idly fishing and it was my job to send them home with something they could cook up into a tasty meal. Sometimes, though, it was us who got the tasty meal. Certain visiting journalists were considered sufficiently important for them to be taken to lunch either at the staff club or one of the better cafes on campus. This always made for a very pleasant couple of hours chatting and eating up large on Tony's expense account though how much payback we ever got was hard to measure.

10

William came early for Christmas, arriving on December 4, and stayed rather late, leaving on June 27! In that time he found a full-time job, completed a polytechnic hospitality course and lived with us in the Dockside apartment where, for about three months he shared his room with an old school mate called Jason. For a while the two of them were also joined by my nephew David, from Cape Town, who had come to work temporarily in Australia. For the best part of two weeks Maria and I seemed to spend all our time shopping, like a couple of frantic birds bringing food back to the nest for three hungry and very demanding chicks.

Our daughter Emma, who heard at the end of November she'd passed her final exams and was now a fully fledged vet, flew in on December 20 after three weeks on an Outward Bound course. She turned up looking well but tired and was gone a week later, hurrying back across the Tasman to spend New Year with her boyfriend. But coming the other way, to sample New Year Brisbane-style, was our good friend Caroline whom we'd last seen in Paris. Other friends from New Zealand, now only three hours flying time away, also began dropping in, which was lovely after being starved of familiar Kiwi faces while in England. It was shaping up to be a memorable summer: in fact, it turned out to be brilliant, not just the summer but way beyond.

I should mention that Caroline, as well as being a dear friend, is also related by marriage—about five years earlier her golden retriever Sascha had married Buffy. It was among the most memorable weddings ever seen in Blenheim and took place one sunny afternoon in Caroline's garden. There were about 60 guests and 14 other dogs, including one who was a bridesmaid and another who acted as pageboy. One of New Zealand's top organists happened to be staying with other friends that weekend and agreed to perform at the wedding, as did a talented young French horn player from the national youth orchestra. Another friend, a genuine marriage celebrant, arrived by rickshaw to conduct the ceremony which concluded with an exchange of rings—in this case doughnuts which were eagerly consumed before they could be placed on respective paws, Sascha somehow managing to wolf both of them despite the hindrance of a rose-petal covered veil.

The mothers of the happy couple and myself were all rather startlingly dressed for the occasion after popping down to the local theatre to hire outfits instead of going to Moss Bros. Guests sang songs, there was an enormous wedding cake, untold food and booze, and the whole event was captured for posterity on video. For some people the wedding no doubt confirmed their worst suspicions about the Nelsons' sanity. But the truth is several people came up to us afterwards and said this was the best wedding they had ever been to. Not only that but a few others who we forgot to invite were pretty annoyed with us when they found out what they'd missed.

Everyone who visited us in Dockside fell in love with the place. Our apartment was comfortable and spacious, with great views, but it was the rest of the hotel and the surrounding complex which really made an impression. Living in a bustling, upmarket hotel is exciting. We got to know the staff on reception as there was almost always someone there whenever we came in or went out. Often we'd share the lift with a bright young person delivering food or drinks to one of the rooms while 24 hours a day security men prowled around the hotel's public areas and the grounds. Just about every week night the hotel hosted one or more gatherings in its meeting rooms, anything from groups of insurance sales people or company shareholders to young revellers at a 21st birthday disco. Then, at weekends, it was the turn of wedding parties to gather around the complex, sometimes for the ceremony itself but usually for some pretty swanky receptions.

Leaning over our balcony we looked almost straight down on Chinos, a smart little inside-outside cafe, all terracotta tiles, tinkling fountains, comfy sofas, racks of newspapers and magazines. And great food. Chinos became almost a second home—certainly a second dining room—as we succumbed to a weakness for wood-fired tandoori pizzas with salad followed by lemon meringue pie. Next door to Chinos was the Comedy Club, a great venue for stand-up comedians while bands also played there at weekends. We became regulars at this club which attracted some outstanding Australian comics. Vince Sorrenti was probably the best of the bunch. He had everyone in stitches with his tales of Aussie life through Italian immigrant eyes, beginning with how his early efforts to fit in were undermined by his Italian mother who insisted on sending him off to primary school every day with extremely ripe parmesan sandwiches. However, this club was also the scene of one of our most excruciatingly awful nights when we made the mistake of attending the heats of a local talent competition for stand-up comics.

There were something like 10 aspiring comedians on the bill and at least nine of them were embarrassingly and completely dreadful. Several died a terrible death but sadly didn't realise it and ploughed on digging themselves deeper and deeper into the mire. We once heard an American consumer advocate saying you should always complain if there's something wrong with the service you get, your meal in a restaurant or the goods you buy. She said a complaint should be seen as a gift to the person responsible because it makes them aware of a problem and enables them to put it right. Before I walked out of this appalling show at the interval, someone in the audience delivered a small but beautifully wrapped gift. One of the "comedians", having run out of obscene and extremely unfunny jokes, had resorted to doing impressions of parts of the body, most of them below the waist. "What am I?" he kept asking until finally being put out of his misery by a gruff Liverpudlian voice which piped up: "You're absolute shite." Ah, what a perfect present that was.

Immediately around the hotel were several other newer apartment blocks and various amenities which together gave the appearance of a freshly washed and laundered toytown. Within 50 yards of the front door were a couple of restaurants and a small but well-stocked, well-patronised convenience store somewhat incongruously called Peter's Palace. Close by there was also a hairdresser's and beauty salon, a small wine shop, two estate agents offices, a large outdoor pool, two floodlit tennis courts and a gym.

For several years in Blenheim Maria and I had gone regularly to the local gym and played quite a bit of tennis. However, for the past 18 months virtually our only exercise had been walking dogs. Better than nothing but not enough to stop some extra padding attaching itself to our midriffs. It was also a question of keeping up energy levels: the strange thing about exercise is that the more energy you expend, the more you seem to have. So we signed up at the Dockside gym, reasoning that although it was a little more expensive than others in the city centre, we would use it more as it was right on our doorstep. And so it proved. For the next six months we probably averaged four to five sessions a week at the gym, in my case mostly straight after work and at weekends. It was only a small gym but well equipped and it was right next to the outdoor pool. We made full use of this wonderful facility, mostly in the slightly cooler mornings and evenings, gently swimming up and down and lazily flicking away fallen frangipani blossoms. At such times 340 dollars didn't seem a bad price to pay…

We hadn't seen the kids for six months and when they jetted in on the wings of our frequent flyer air miles it was great to catch up again. As in Melbourne, the Christmas weather was hot and sunny, hardly what we had grown up with when kids ourselves in the northern hemisphere. So there was no traditional roast turkey with all the trimmings—instead we settled for an Xmas breakfast on the balcony with scrambled eggs, bacon, smoked salmon and avocado, washed down with bubbly and orange juice. Occasionally Maria or I have had to work on Christmas Day, but not this year. Instead, for the first time in living memory, it was our son's turn, and he headed downstairs to the restaurant at 11am to begin setting up for Christmas lunch. We heartily sympathised with him for all of 30 seconds and then spent the rest of the day swimming, reading, walking, playing with a new chess set and, of course, eating. Boxing Day was similar although Emma, hunting for a wedding outfit, insisted on dragging us all down town to Myers department store where we joined 71,000 other shoppers for the opening day of the summer sales. Despite my initial protests I ended up buying more things than Emma and Maria put together which was a bit of a worry.

Within Dockside Hotel itself were two restaurants, Captain's Cove and Snug Harbour. The latter was where yachts used to tie up on the river just a stone's throw from the lovely outside dining area, where a great folk and blues guitarist played in the shade on Sunday afternoons…and where William was lucky enough to land a job. He walked into the restaurant shortly after arriving, flashed his fairly lean CV and within a couple of days was waiting tables on a late shift. Decked out in black trousers, white shirt and black bow tie, all from the local op shop, a black apron and a pair of my black shoes, he was soon in demand for various shifts during the day and at night. One of his trump cards was being Johnny on the spot—having to commute just 12 floors straight down by lift meant he was always available to fill in if other staff went sick or failed to turn up. He worked mostly in Snug Harbour but also did occasional shifts in Chinos. The work was pretty well paid, sometimes there were reasonable tips—mostly from Americans who came off the yachts at the bottom of the garden—and there was the added bonus of free or half price food. Needless to say, the amount of cake and other goodies transported from Chinos to our apartment increased enormously.

The approach of Christmas had been a very mellow time at the university with everyone even more relaxed than usual, office decorations up, and cakes, biscuits and chocolates mysteriously appearing in the tea room. One vitally important tradition that did keep us on our toes was the graduation ceremonies held in the week before Christmas. With many hundreds of people graduating there was no shortage of good human-interest stories—mothers and daughters graduating together, twins, disabled people, a reformed jailbird receiving his degree and many others. I attended a couple of the ceremonies. At one there was a huge roar as a young blind woman went up on stage to receive her degree accompanied by her golden labrador guide dog. Her mother had made the dog's jacket in the same colours as her daughter's gown.

The university also dished out several honorary degrees, one on this occasion to actor Geoffrey Rush. Well-known from such films as *Shakespeare in Love* and *Elizabeth*, Rush was at this time basking in the celebrity of having recently won an Oscar for best actor for his performance in the movie *Shine*. I was part of the small welcoming committee from our department meeting Rush beforehand. He was a very pleasant guy and happy to be back at his alma mater but clearly also extremely nervous, sucking down cigarettes at an alarming rate. However, once on stage he visibly relaxed, despite having to wear that daft floppy bonnet, and delivered a very entertaining speech about his days at UQ and the road he has travelled since to Hollywood stardom.

By this time of year the campus had become comparatively deserted. Which was great! Vacation time meant no more jostling through the usual thick crowds of ravenous young people every lunchtime, no more queuing in cafes, at the bank or in shops. At the same time lots of staff headed away on their summer breaks, many deliberately not leaving any contact phone numbers or addresses. I didn't blame them as no doubt they had fully earned their peace and quiet. But it did make things a bit tricky in our office. Lots of reporters and writers, scratching for stories during the "silly season", that traditionally quiet news time over Christmas and through January, were looking for experts to talk to on a wide variety of issues just to help fill space.

Considering I had been at the university only just over a month, I was pretty pleased to land an 11-day break from Christmas Eve through to January 5. Maria also had a few days off but was lured back to the hospital partly because they were so short of registered nurses and partly by the very handsome pay rates for working weekends and public holidays during this time. Brisbane had some wonderful things organized for the festive season, one of the highlights being the Night the River Sings, a magical river parade of illuminated boats combined with singing and music. We were out on one of the small water taxis on our way to a good vantage point when we became caught up in the parade. As a result we found ourselves accidentally occupying the best seats in the house, watching on the water as the colourful convoy of boats slowly motored past us and then enjoying a superb display of fireworks right overhead.

Brisbane loves its fireworks. There were huge displays at Southbank virtually every night around Christmas and into January. Often we'd see them lighting up the sky from wherever we happened to be around the city but we also got the most fantastic views from our balcony. Most times we'd be inside with the air conditioning turned up when we'd hear the distant pop and fizz, the signal to take our coffee out on to the balcony and sit there enjoying the show. The other fantastic display we used to watch from the balcony was provided by Mother Nature—electrical storms. After very hot and humid weather these fiery displays of lightning would rake the night sky with dazzling fingers of brilliant white light. Sometimes there was thunder too and every once in a while Brisbane would have the most amazing rain storms. We would watch these rolling in from the inland plains, accompanied by increasing winds and sharply decreasing temperatures. Then the rain would arrive. Heavy, relentless, battering rain falling in thick sheets, cutting visibility and causing numerous minor flash floods. Next morning leaves and other debris on the ground might mark the extent of the storm but invariably it was hot and sunny again and everything was already dry.

There was a good storm the day Emma left. We could see it building in the sky as I drove her to the airport. It struck Brisbane a few miles away and then came howling over the flat plains towards the airport, arriving minutes after her plane had safely taken off and climbed above the weather. But earlier that morning I had put some washing out to dry on the balcony, a process which normally took around 15 minutes. By the time I got home the storm had gone and so had all the washing—shirts, socks, shorts, towels, there was nothing left. I searched all around the hotel grounds down below but my things had probably landed miles away and I never found a trace of them.

From our balcony we also used to watch some wonderful wildlife, including pairs of sea eagles which would patrol the river, circle around the rooftops of neighbouring apartment blocks and cavort together high overhead. It was from the balcony that we saw our one and only Australian snake—not ON the balcony, I hasten to add, but far below on one of the lawns. We wouldn't normally have seen it from that distance but when a noisy crowd gathered we grabbed our binoculars and saw this skinny brown thing about two feet long. Whatever it was, it evidently wasn't too dangerous as one of the hotel staff appeared with a pizza box, scooped up the reptile with a rather nonchalant flourish and took it away.

But when it came to Brisbane wildlife, the biggest attraction for us were the bats—thousands of huge flying foxes which came flooding out of their roosts at dusk every night and flapped silently over the city looking to drain the blood from young virgins while they slept. Ah, sorry, forget about the blood and the virgins, got a bit carried away there. But the rest is true and the bats really are an incredible natural phenomenon. In our first flat on Kangaroo Point we could hear and see them squealing away in palm trees right outside our balcony. But from the Dockside apartment, around 7pm throughout the summer, we would watch them emerging in the distant tropical twilight like a long, continuous wisp of smoke. Though they would eat certain fruits they were searching primarily for nectar and hundreds would flap through the darkening sky past our balcony, some just a few feet above our heads, on their way to feast in the Botanic Gardens across the river. At the university I wrote a few stories about Brisbane's bats, the largest of which can weigh upwards of two pounds. There are several varieties in this part of Queensland, some of which are becoming endangered as they suffer at the hands of unsympathetic fruit farmers and find their natural habitats slowly disappearing.

Caroline flew in on New Year's Eve bringing an eclectic range of goodies with her—wonderful sauvignon blanc wine from our home province of Marlborough, fudge, photos of our dog, plus cards and messages from friends. We went back to Dockside ostensibly to relax and have a bite to eat but instead spent the next several hours talking flat out. William was again working and Emma was back in New Zealand, so Caroline, Maria and I made our way through the gathering crowds to Southbank. Brisbane has a very manageable population of just over one million and they all seemed to have brought a friend to greet the new year. We managed to squeeze into a restaurant for supper and then found a spot on the river bank with a great view of the midnight fireworks, an incredibly coordinated display with some launched from a barge in the water and others from the roofs of the city's highest buildings.

Just over three weeks later Brisbanites were at it again, celebrating one of the major public holidays, Australia Day, with a free concert in the Botanic Gardens and various other attractions topped off with several more tons of fireworks. The day is marked in countless ways around the country and one of the sporting highlights in Brisbane turned out to be the 17th annual cockroach races at the Story Bridge Hotel. There is, of course, no shortage of these browny black beetle-like insects in Brisbane, the leathery little devils living in every nook and cranny and scurrying out at night to eat whatever they can find. They had successfully colonised our small tea room at the university and proved remarkably resistant to regular bouts of fumigation. Cockroaches, creepy critters with few friends, have never enjoyed a very good press but even so it was hard to see how they deserved this annual "sporting" abuse.

Before each race about a dozen cockies had numbers written on their backs before being dropped into an empty beer jug that was tipped upside down inside a circle. People could bet on their favourite roach and when the jug was lifted, the first one to make it outside the circle was declared the winner. By the time we arrived, around 3pm, it was stinking hot and just about everyone there was well and truly sozzled. Some big bets and bigger beers were going down, and the noise accompanying each race was deafening. And so the final race, the "Cockroach Crunch", probably came as a blessed relief to the last of the competitors which, when the jug was removed, were quickly pulverised under stomping work boots and jandals before they had a chance to drown in all that spilled beer.

Things were pretty quiet at the university straight after the holiday and it was the same in the restaurant business, prompting William to take a short-lived second job trying to persuade people to sell their houses and cars through the Internet. He earned $10 an hour with a rather dubious-sounding $5 bonus if the customer paid there and then using a credit card. However, within a week or two he was in demand again downstairs and had also embarked on his 14-week hospitality course at one of the Brisbane polytechnics. This signalled the start of some long days for him—class sessions ran from 9am until 2pm which gave him just enough time to rush home, change and fly downstairs for the 3pm to 11pm shift. The course covered all aspects of bar work, waitering and restaurant management, and the final certificate was to prove extremely useful over the next year or so.

Meanwhile Maria, always keen to expand her horizons and stop the old grey matter solidifying, had also signed up for a polytech course on computers. This covered a wide range of skills, including some pretty complicated stuff such as spreadsheets. Whenever someone was stuck they had to place a red cone on top of their machine and wait for the tutor to come round and help them. I think she might have regretted telling me about that as for a long time afterwards I would tease her about red cones if she had trouble with the simplest of tasks from taking the top off the ketchup to finding her keys.

About this time an old friend from Blenheim, who had been living in Brisbane several years, decided she was going on a three-month trip to the UK and offered us her car while she was away. It was the first time we'd had regular use of a car for almost two years and though we really didn't need one in Brisbane, we decided to make the most of it. We hardly used it around the city, much preferring to travel by boat, but did begin venturing further afield at weekends, especially up and down the Queensland coast. Not ALL the way up and down the Queensland coast, I must add. Queensland covers a massive area and like so many parts of Australia is a region where driving is measured in days rather than miles.

As it was, our excursions hardly registered on the map. We would head a couple of hours northwards to the Sunshine Coast and the surfing mecca of Noosa; or maybe swing inland slightly to the Glasshouse mountains, extraordinary, 20 million-year-old lumps of rock which are visible for miles around, including far out to sea, as they jut up from the board-flat landscape. Or we might turn south from Brisbane towards the Gold Coast where another couple of friends from New Zealand have settled. They live near the top of one of those soaring towers where the rooms offer incredible sweeping views over miles of sea, surf and golden sands in one direction, rivers, plains and mountains in another. And it was here one memorable day we had our first—and I must admit rather addictive—taste of casino gambling.

Our friends enjoyed just playing for small stakes on the slot machines and one day they took us with them to Conrad's Jupiter Casino, affectionately known thereafter as Uncle Con. We only had a few dollars which we split between us and went our separate ways. For some reason Maria started playing poker machines and ended up winning about $100. Which was quite remarkable as Maria has absolutely no idea how to play poker. She is, in fact, the world's worst card player and to my certain knowledge has never mastered any game more complicated than Happy Families. Countless times I have tried to explain the basics of games like bridge, blackjack and poker, and just when I think she's got it she'll say something like: "Now what are these little black clover things called again?" Or, after betting heavily and with commendable inscrutability throughout a hand of draw poker, she'll lay down something like a queen high and then look totally flabbergasted as all her money is raked away. I never saw her playing the casino poker machines and can only assume her complete lack of logic seriously undermined the confidence of the machine's micro-chip.

I was in another part of the cool and pleasantly smoke-free casino playing something called a Keno machine where I had to select random numbers between one and 80. Naturally I was doing so using incredible skill harnessed to scientific and statistically proven methods based on such things as the dog's age and the childrens' birthdays. By the time we were all reunited I had managed to come out about 60 bucks ahead. So, great celebrations all round and pleasant wonderment at finding just how easy it is to make money gambling. Next day we popped back and, bubbling with confidence now, increased our stakes. After an hour we had lost half the previous day's winnings and would probably have been cleaned out if we hadn't had to go home. After that we used to enjoy an occasional flutter in a sister casino in Brisbane. We kept the stakes low and usually played the same one or two favourite machines but even so it wasn't long before Uncle Con had all his money back, with interest.

Another trip we did in "our" new car was a weekend away at Toowoomba. This gracious little town, a couple of hours by road from Brisbane, was built more than 2,000 feet up on the edge of the Great Dividing Range. It was once a fashionable and certainly cooler retreat for Queensland's well-to-do who would travel there to escape the searing heat of Brisbane and the lowland plains. Our reason for going there was no less cool—we went to see a real blast from the past, the Barron Knights. If you were around in the '60s you might remember this group whose fame and fortune was based on their cheeky comedy take-offs of the singers and hit songs of that era. These days, like a number of groups which were once household names but have long since disappeared from most radar screens, they are still making a good living touring the world. They turn up regularly in places like Hong Kong,

Sri Lanka, New Zealand and Toowoomba, and still put on a surprisingly entertaining show. But what was really amazing about the Barron Knights was that two or three band members were survivors from the original line-up 38 years ago.

We were always trying to get to as many films and as much live music and theatre as possible in Brisbane, recognising the opportunities would never be quite so thick on the ground once we came to settle back in Blenheim. This led us to take another trip down memory lane, not long after the Barron Knights, when we went to see *All You Need is Beatles*, a musical tribute to the Fab Four led by their one-time record producer George (now Sir George) Martin. He conducted the hugely enthusiastic and talented Queensland State Youth Orchestra which was joined by various other artists in a wonderful two and a half hours of Beatles music. While the music was truly magnificent, for many the highlights of the concert were the personal reminiscences of Sir George and the little stories he told between numbers about working with Paul, John, George and Ringo.

Maria, who had been slaving away much of this time with geriatric patients, was delighted to start picking up some casual but fairly regular shifts at the university's student health clinic. After dealing with decaying old wrinklies she just loved the contrast of suddenly seeing bouncy, energetic young patients whose average age must have been all of 19. Their medical needs were considerably more exciting—plenty of sex-related matters, of course, and other interesting cases of people either coming from or going to unusual parts of the world, so either bringing in exotic ailments or trying to ward them off. On days Maria worked at the health clinic we would take the Cat together and try to meet for lunch. Sometimes for a treat we'd go somewhere like Wordsmiths, a cafe-cum-bookshop with lovely but rather pricey food, often accompanied by book readings and signings. Or else we'd go distinctly downmarket and eat in one of the student cafeterias, an environment much more in keeping with our status as budget travellers.

At lunchtimes the campus was always thronging with students and it was fun just wandering about soaking up the non-stop carnival atmosphere. Invariably stalls would spring up on the grass or in court-yards selling virtually the same things that were being hawked a world away on the Liverpool campus when I was a student there more than 30 years before. Music tapes and records, paperback books, posters (good to see Che Guevara still going strong), retro clothes, cheap food and membership of organisations promising everything from saved whales to legalised pot to all-out revolution.

Something else we found out about by accident and which then became a regular fixture was a one-man weekly organic food market. This took place every Thursday in a carpark behind the physics build-ing: it was small scale but had obviously built up a loyal clientele who arrived from all corners of the campus carrying their own shopping bags. All the produce was very cheap and interesting. A tad wary the first time, we just bought mandarins and avocados which were weighed out on rickety scales in the back of an equally rickety old van. But they were mouth-wateringly superb. From then on we bought a little of vir-tually everything on offer and were seldom disappointed. The chap who grew the produce and ran the market was very green and was con-ducting something of a crusade against seed companies who, he reck-oned, were responsible for the virtual extinction of many rare varieties. His mission was trying to save and promote those threatened species and at his urging we tried a variety of cabbage that was popular in the 17th century. It was nice enough but cabbage doesn't appear to have changed much over three hundred years...

Around the campus there was almost always some free entertain-ment going on. One day our cafeteria lunch was spiced up by belly dancers and another time we went to the music department to hear a classical guitarist. We concluded that the young man playing, who came from somewhere in central Europe, could not speak English. He certainly didn't utter a single word throughout, not even to introduce pieces or acknowledge the audience applause, which gave his performance a rather eerie edge.

Even on quiet days with nothing special happening, the Great Court never failed to inspire. Students poured through the main entrance, beneath a chiselled inscription reading "Great is truth and mighty above all things", and peeled off left or right around the cool, echoing sandstone cloisters. In the centre was a huge grass area where students would sit or lie, talk, study or sleep, often in the shade of jacaranda trees whose vivid purply-blue flowers stunned the senses in early springtime and summer.

The stories I was writing led me to every corner of the university and I also started taking a few photographs, something I had not done since working as a branch office journalist in New Zealand several years previously. With such a wealth of subjects to cover I was never bored for a minute. I wrote about research into the health benefits of owning pets and about modern terrorism; I spoke to a professor on the likely effects of the Millennium computer bug and to a vet who had opened a canine cancer clinic; I interviewed a newly-appointed high court judge, an 82-year-old graduate and a PhD student writing a thesis on the vital role of bats as tree pollinators; I discovered how computers are making it easier to learn foreign languages and how Vietnam veterans are being helped to cope with stress. I filed stories about health, pop music, children, people writing books, physics, pharmacy and pathology, insects, social work, romance languages, the solar system and sport in South Africa. The variety was endless. I even wrote publicity for a thanksgiving service held each year to acknowledge those who donate their bodies for university research.

The academics and other staff I came across were mostly a great bunch but they shared a common gripe—they were always complaining about the lack of money available for education. Many remembered the good old days when workloads were light, holidays long and there were buckets of cash for universities. Their beef now was that everyone had to work a great deal harder and fight for every dollar from a rapidly diminishing pool. I murmured my sympathies but couldn't help thinking: "Welcome to the real world." As far as I could tell, university staff were still leading a sheltered and privileged existence compared to their counterparts in private enterprise. Even in our very modest department, for example, taxi chittys were readily available for trips off campus and nobody ever batted an eyelid at $50 or $60 round trips. Most newspapers I know of would be looking twice at such casual spending and asking why the journalist hadn't a) taken their own car, b) caught a bus, or c) just picked up the phone.

It was high summer and hot in Brisbane, and almost everyone was sensibly dressed very casually. I often found it difficult to tell the difference between the professors I went to interview and their students: the dress codes were decidedly similar, the professors, perhaps, just a few years older. In the midst of all this tanned flesh, I remained a rather buttoned down, over-dressed Pom. I had worn a suit and tie for the interview and somehow just kept on turning up that way until scaling back slightly to casual trousers and a sports jacket. Admittedly I took to carrying the jacket and loosening my tie in an effort to ward off heat exhaustion—even in winter we were toasting in temperatures up to 25 degrees. But even so I still stood out from colleagues with their shorts, open-necked shirts and sandals. One day at work we took part in Jeans Day, a nationwide fund-raiser for some good cause or other, when people paid $5 to wear jeans to the office or $10 if they didn't turn up in jeans. I had to pay $10 as my only jeans were back in New Zealand. The irony was that my heavy English suit and sports jacket together had cost less than the average pair of jeans.

How so? Elementary, my dear Watson. Op shops. Opportunity shops and charity shops are now everywhere in England, usually half a dozen or more per main street, and obviously a great source of revenue for the organisations which run them. Maria and I have become regular customers and among my best buys were the heavy worsted suit, plus an extra pair of trousers, all for a fiver, and the herringbone sports coat costing eight pounds. Maria has also kitted herself out several times over, spending relatively few pounds on bagfuls of clothes she'll cheerfully chuck out a few months later. Oddly enough William, once the budding Steptoe of the family, now turns his nose up at second-hand and instead buys quite expensive new clothes. All this is a far cry from some of the posh places we've looked after as Animal Aunts where couples often have "his" and "hers" walk-in closets full of hand-made shirts, suits and shoes, and racks of designer dresses. One particular client had so much stuff she employed a woman to come in three times a week just to sort out her clothes. One day this woman spent an entire morning just going through the shoes, a job which, in our case, would take all of 30 seconds.

While I was at UQ, plans began to take shape for relocating the public relations department. It was to move lock, stock and two smoking barrels from the second floor of the J. D. Story administration building to the seventh and top floor. Planning was well under way by May even though the shift was not due for at least another six months. There were strong and decidedly mixed feelings about the move. Even this early in the proceedings people were frantically jockeying for position, trying to stake their claim for the best, biggest and brightest office space. Since I wasn't going to be around I could sit back as a neutral observer and watch as office politics reared its ugly head. An increasing amount of staff time began to be devoted to informal talks and full-blown committee meetings to thrash out such thorny topics as colour schemes, types of filing cabinets and other furniture, the position of power points and phone plugs, and even the colour of the office coffee mugs.

By an interestingly coincidence, 12 months later I was working in the corresponding department at the University of Colorado, in Boulder, and they were going through exactly the same exercise. There the department was moving to a different building, the working party committee meetings were in full swing, minutes were being circulated and basically the Yanks were grappling with the same issues as their Aussie counterparts. I don't recall coffee mugs being mentioned while I was there, though no doubt that cropped up subsequently, but the Americans were just as keen on in-depth debate when it came to furniture lay-out and colour charts.

And talking of Yanks, all this time we had been moving slowly but surely—and with no shortage of headaches—towards securing our American green cards. Admittedly some of the complications were of our own making. We had begun the application process with the American embassy in Auckland but naturally wanted to switch the whole thing to Sydney once we moved to Australia. However, we had to have medicals and then interviews and were worried that changing countries like this could push our case further back in the queue and jeopardise our chances of laying hands on the holy green grail. So began an intense few weeks of faxes and phone calls around the Brisbane/Auckland/Sydney triangle. Okay, they finally said, you can have your medicals in Brisbane, the interview in Sydney, plus you'll need Australian police checks and fingerprints along with photographs for the eventual green cards.

The mug shots had to satisfy a whole list of very precise conditions regarding such things as size, angle of the head and background colour. A couple of cold beers were enough to bribe one of the university's media photographers to take them. But I wondered afterwards if perhaps we should have paid hard cash instead as my photo was absolutely terrible and on my green card I now resemble a 78-year-old recent stroke victim. Why is it photos for official documents always look so embarrassingly awful? Desperate to avoid another such debacle, I recently used a 15-year-old photograph of me with a beard on a new driving licence. Probably highly illegal but at least now I won't break out into a vanity-fuelled but still highly suspicious cold sweat if anyone asks to see my licence.

It turned out there was only one doctor in the whole of Brisbane who was certified by the American embassy to carry out the medicals. Boy, is he on a good number. The examination was especially perfunctory—a few basic questions about heart attacks and insanity, a sketchy physical (tap on knee, breath in…out, thank you), and that was it. Oh, apart from forking out his $150 fee. This was followed by blood tests ($110 each) and chest X-rays, a snip at $67, leaving us a total of $654 out of pocket. We had also completed the necessary police checks and fingerprinting and (a clever touch, we thought) obtained a glowing reference together with a statement of assets from our bank in Blenheim.

The US embassy in Sydney wrote calling us for interview on May 6 but the letter only arrived a week beforehand which didn't really give us enough notice. We tried to put it back a few weeks to fit in with our travel plans to New Zealand but in the end had to accept a compromise date of May 13. The interview worried us more than anything and we carefully rehearsed some sugary answers to what we thought were likely questions. We nervously imagined ourselves sitting under a bright light in a darkened room while a battery of grizzled ex-FBI agents fired tough, searching questions at us and cold-eyed psychiatrists analysed our every answer and body language. In the end, of course, it was nothing like that. In fact it was hardly what you'd call an interview at all. We stood on the very public side of what looked like two inches of bullet-proof glass and answered a couple of innocuous questions through a speaker system which amplified everything being said for the benefit of all the people in the waiting area. Indeed, while we were waiting our turn we followed with interest the unsuccessful case being put forward by a man trying to secure a visa so his Mexican girlfriend could visit him in the States.

The whole process of checking our applications, having the "interview" and handing over the fee of around $1,200 probably took no more than half an hour. But then came one of the most ludicrous things we have ever encountered anywhere in the world. The green cards have to be sent out several weeks later to wherever the applicant is in the United States but the embassy, which is 15 floors up in a central Sydney office block, does not provide envelopes. So we had to go 15 floors down to street level, find a newsagents, buy an envelope, come back up 15 floors, through the airport-like security check and back to the counter. Ah, they said without so much as a flickering eyelid, you also need a stamp.

Now, if it had been anything else but our green cards we would probably have inquired sweetly why they didn't already provide effing envelopes and sodding stamps since they must know exactly what size envelopes and how much postage is required. It also seemed to us perfectly reasonable that our $1,200 fee could, at the very least, have covered the cost of a stamped envelope. However, having come this far we weren't about to upset Uncle Sam now. So we said nothing and meekly retraced our steps down 15 floors to ground level, round several corners to the post office, back up, through security and handed over a stamp to the stony-faced clerk who had no doubt seen it all before. By the time we finally left the embassy we were so elated at getting the green cards we could only laugh at this quirky little example of American bureaucracy. As we were to find out later, it was pretty much par for the course when dealing with US government departments, especially immigration and the IRS.

11

After the embassy visit we stayed another night in Sydney before flying across the Tasman for our annual return to New Zealand. Besides catching up with everyone again our major goal over the next two weeks was to attend Emma's graduation at Massey University, in the middle of the North Island, on May 22. Since leaving university a few months earlier Emma had been looking for a job but there was very little around at the time. In fact things seemed so unpromising in New Zealand she was on the point of accepting an offer from a clinic in Adelaide, South Australia. She had long since decided large animals were not for her; or, as Maria so quaintly told everyone, she didn't want to spend the rest of her working life with her arm up a cow's bum. Then, at the 11th hour, she heard of a job going at a small animal clinic in Christchurch. The day after her 23rd birthday she flew south to Christchurch for the interview, spayed a couple of cats and was offered the job on the spot. She worked there almost exactly two years, gaining valuable practical experience, before heading for England and lucrative times as a locum.

We still kept in close contact with everyone back in Marlborough but from afar had no way of judging how deeply the community had been affected by the disappearance and murder of two local young people. Ben Smart, 21, and his friend Olivia Hope, 17, had gone missing while attending New Year's Eve celebrations in the Marlborough Sounds. The Sounds are a labyrinth of waterways at the top of the South Island, popular with holidaymakers and boaties, and an annual magnet for young people looking to party in the New Year. Like so many others in the relatively tight-knit Blenheim and Marlborough community, we knew both the families. Via the Internet in Australia we followed the agonising search for the missing youngsters which began almost immediately and lasted for many months.

No trace of them has ever been found but in June police arrested Scott Watson and 12 months later the case finally came to trial. Watson pleaded not guilty to murder and has continued to protest his innocence but he was convicted and sentenced to life in prison with a minimum non-parole period of 17 years. When we arrived in mid-May this crime, which had dominated the media for more than four months, was still uppermost in everyone's mind. People were in sombre mood, many still shocked and finding it hard to accept that two young people, out having fun in such an idyllic spot, had met such a sudden and violent end.

We stayed in Blenheim just a week but somehow managed to pack in all the business we needed to do. This time people had very conveniently organised a couple of parties for us which brought everyone together under one roof and made the catching up that much easier. Naturally we saw as much as possible of Buffy and were pleased to find our house still standing. In fact the house and our large, rambling garden were looking extremely well cared for. Everything seemed to have grown like topsy and we made a mental note that some of our many trees would soon need trimming—four years later they're still waiting.

We rummaged through boxes, drawers and piles of stuff in our locked front room, dumping a few bits and pieces and taking away odd items of clothing to refresh our tired-looking wardrobes. This whole exercise took much longer than expected as we kept discovering interesting things we had forgotten we still had. When we eventually settle down there again and go through all our belongings it will be like unwrapping presents on Christmas morning. We had lunch one day with our tenants who had recently started their own business in Blenheim. This was good news for us as we imagined their capital would be tied up for a while and not available to fritter on something so frivolous as their own home! They certainly seemed happy to keep renting our place for another year or so while their business became established and we were really happy to have them.

After tidying up the usual official stuff with the bank, accountant, insurance company and the local council, seeing our property man Bob and spending time with former work colleagues, it was time to head north. We caught a ferry across Cook Strait to Wellington and then drove up to Massey, the only university in New Zealand which offers veterinary science. It soon became apparent our social whirl had not ended in Blenheim. We discovered we knew some of the other proud parents staying at the same motel and that night we caught up with various other old friends from around the country at a pre-graduation dinner…another reminder of just how small New Zealand is. In addition to all this, our daughter's boyfriend was also graduating so we had a chance to meet his parents for the first time, plus loads of Emma's friends who until then we had only heard her talking about.

It was a struggle to be in our places at Palmerston North's Regent Theatre by 8.30 next morning but we were wide awake by the time proceedings started at 9am. It was a beautiful ceremony and considerably quieter and more dignified than several subsequent ones I have attended in the United States. When I worked at the University of Colorado, graduation ceremonies were held in the campus football stadium which probably accounted for the extremely vocal and unruly football-like crowd that officials seemed powerless to control. The ceremony, short on dignity and long on hoopla, also lacked the personal touch. In New Zealand and Australia students walked up on stage to be individually congratulated and presented with their degrees; in Boulder that was all done en masse with great sections of the crowd standing up at a time to be acknowledged by a speaker 75 yards away out in the arena.

After the formalities for Emma and her peers, everyone adjourned for a mammoth photo session a few miles away on the university campus where the sunshine and autumn colours made conditions perfect for pictures. It was a memorable day for our daughter and lovely for us to be there sharing it with her.

We flew back to Australia like royalty. I don't mean first class…I mean in separate planes. I tracked down a cheap deal with Air New Zealand while Maria hopped on Qantas a couple of days later using her frequent flyer miles. I would have joined her but my own air points were looking a bit moth-eaten after the kids' Christmas visits.

Almost immediately we began looking for a new flat. Our motivation was primarily financial—Dockside, though fantastic, was a heavy drain on the purse—but also practical—William was leaving in a few weeks so we couldn't really go on justifying a two-bedroom apartment. The main areas we looked at were across the river by the Botanic Gardens and in Chinatown. At the tip of Kangaroo Point was Story Bridge, a wonderful steel latticework structure built in 1940. It was a great bridge, beautiful when lit up at night, and when we walked across it we could feel it shuddering and shaking as trucks and buses thundered past. Water taxis, CityCats and other boats sailed under its massive arches looking like bath toys from above as we walked towards Chinatown in search of cheap Chinese meals or on one of our regular forays to The Healer, a former church now used as a folk/blues/country music club.

Chinatown was a buzzy place, full of colourful shops and restaurants, and we seriously looked a several flats there. However, they were not that much cheaper than Dockside and certainly didn't offer nearly as much for the money, so we decided to stay put a little longer until the end of June when William was returning to New Zealand. Then, quite unexpectedly, we found what we were looking for in an area we hadn't really considered—St Lucia, right by the university. The Manors was a brand new, low-rise development built in a square around an outdoor pool and barbecue area. It was so new some units were still being finished off and furnished when we first went to have a look around. We signed up on a first-floor, one-bedroom apartment on

June 12, paid our deposit on June 24 and moved in the first week of July, perfect timing for us.

From our windows we could look out across the tops of trees and playing fields to glimpse some of the university buildings. My office was less than 10 minutes walk away. Sadly that meant no more commuting by catamaran and leisurely book reading morning and night; but on the plus side I could have almost another hour in bed in the morning, pop home for lunch if I wanted and save the cost of those monthly season tickets. Most important of all, the weekly rent was $210, so $130 a week cheaper than Dockside. We now had about three months left in Brisbane before putting those green cards to work and needed to start some serious saving. We reckoned the lower rent alone would leave around another $1,500 in our pockets...in theory of course.

In practice, being right on the doorstep of the university, to say nothing of the tasty little restaurants and high-calorie cafes which occupy 90 percent of St Lucia, meant there were other spending temptations we couldn't always resist. The suburb of St Lucia never strays far from the river. Everywhere seems very Mediterranean; the place is very sunny, green and leafy, and teeming with colourful birds—kookaburras, rosellas, magpies, butcherbirds, rainbow lorikeets, friarbirds, corellas, galahs and something aptly called the noisy miner. It's also home to some impressive-sized lizards which, when not basking immobile somewhere, crackle their way through dried-up leaves and twigs looking for lunch.

Not far from St Lucia I found the most amazing Italian barber. Now to be perfectly honest I must admit I'm going just a little thin on top; in fact there are cue balls on *Pot Black* that have more of a thatch than me. Normally Maria gets to deal with this endangered natural resource while I sit self-consciously out in the garden with a towel draped round my shoulders. So it wasn't Pierro's hairdressing skills which attracted me—it was the wonderful way he had with the English language.

Between infrequent customers Pierro, who must have been about 80, would sit at a table outside his shop playing cards with a few pals and drinking small cups of jet black coffee. Wherever he learned his heavily accented English they must have been taught to insert the F-word if they couldn't think of anything else to say. As a result it was effing everything. For example, I was patiently sitting there one day having my nose hair thinned when a young man popped his head in the door. "Eya, fuckin' Carlo, 'ow youafuckin' doin'? I see yourafuckin' girlfriend yesterday. Aah, she's afuckin' beautiful. You gottafuckin' bring her rounda ourafuckin' house for the fuckin' dinner someafuckin' timeasoon." The papers by now were full of the Bill Clinton-Monica Lewinsky affair but Pierro couldn't understand what all the fuss was about. Despite his language he was normally a pretty placid sort of character but he did become a little agitated in his defence of Clinton. This was a situation where the President, like any red-blooded male, was considered entirely blameless. Or, as Pierro best expressed it, for once demonstrating a more literal grasp of the F-word: "Is his afuckin' business what ee's afuckin' doing in his owna fuckin' White House."

Initially when we moved to St Lucia Maria still worked some week-ends at the hospital on Kangaroo Point so for a while our commuting roles were reversed: I would walk to work and she would take the City-Cat half an hour along the river. However, she also began doing some agency work at a private hospital called the Wesley not far from St Lucia and continued two days a week with the student health clinic on campus. Before long she had managed to join the bank of casual nurses at the Wesley intensive care unit and completed her four-day orientation in the first week of August. The Wesley was a very swish place with thick carpets, original art on the walls and lovely food in the staff cafeteria. The hospital was only a couple of miles away from our flat at a place called Milton which gave rise to its popular and not wholly undeserved nickname, the Milton Hilton.

We had been in the flat almost a month before the last of our furniture and furnishings were installed. An interior designer called Maddie was in charge of all this and it became an amusing game on our part to see if this woman could get anything right. She had the strangest taste which the owners were apparently quite happy to let her indulge. Things she had installed either didn't work, looked awful or were just totally unsuitable for such a small flat. The last pieces to arrive were a massive wall unit, which was way out of proportion to the rest of the lounge and also managed to block out some of the natural light, and new, thinner couch cushions. The previous ones had been so fat the only way to sit on the couch was to balance a tiny bit of buttock right on the edge. Also there was no telly.

Now this wasn't a major problem for us. Apart from news, sport (in my case) and a handful of regular programmes, we were minimal television watchers. Indeed, when the kids were young we used to hire a television for the winter months and send it back in the summer. There were always great howls of protest for about a week but after that I settled down and started doing other things…um, I mean the kids settled down and started doing other things. Now we found we could sneak up to my office in the evenings or at weekends if there was something we particularly wanted to see, which for me was usually the All Blacks playing rugby. In addition, we began going to loads of films at the ultra-comfy Schonell Theatre where prices were often only about half those of other movie houses in Brisbane. We also discovered, five minutes from the flat, the university's fantastic main library which was usually open until late and where we had free access to the Internet and e-mails, plus overseas papers.

By this stage we were only a couple of months away from leaving Australia and heading for the United States. We had decided to go to a small town (by American standards) called Boulder, in Colorado, purely on the recommendation of a good friend in Blenheim, Mary Jackson. She had lived there for almost a year and raved about the place. Now we had our green cards but didn't have any particular part of America in mind, Boulder sounded like a great place to start. So we began to do some serious research through the university library, most of it on the Web. We researched the University of Colorado at Boulder, various hospitals and health clinics, and the town's main paper, *The Daily Camera*. We also studied other papers looking for jobs, somewhere to live, and for all the other bits and pieces we could soak up to help build a mental picture of the place which was to become our new home.

One thing we did know about Boulder was that, like Denver, it was a mile above sea level. We'd be living at altitude and to help adjust we decided it was time for a major drive to get fit. We had been slipping a bit in recent weeks but now fronted up at the university gym where Maria joined various fat-burning, heart-pumping, aerobic-type classes and I started a serious regime of weights. One evening when I was at the gym a wild possum loped in through the open door, ran around between the machines for a few moments and then dashed outside again. All very Australian. Meanwhile, Maria was also swimming. She is a good swimmer but this was just another in a long list of skills which had somehow passed me by. To put it mildly, I'd never been at all confident in the water, but I decided it was time I learned.

Is there anything sadder than adult learn-to-swim classes? As I stood shivering in tepid water up to my waist, my voluminous swimming shorts, inflated with air, bobbing ridiculously up to the surface, white arms folded across my puny chest, I couldn't think of anything. In the adjacent lanes of the huge indoor pool children were effortlessly cruising up and down, fooling around and chatting as they went, while I was concentrating hard on just staying alive. Helping me do that was Danielle, a fair dinkum Aussie girl clad in a wet suit which accentuated her stout, oakish thighs. I had immediately bonded with her, the way you do with someone you suspect may be called upon to save your life at any moment.

Moving into a new flat in a new area for some insane reason provided the spur I needed to tackle a new challenge, and so I started

Danielle's course of 10 swimming lessons. There were only ever a handful of us in the class, one of whom pulled something during the first lesson and never came back. Another couple in the class, which was supposed to be for beginners, could in fact swim quite well and seemed to come along just to demoralise me. Surviving the first three lessons I was surprised to notice some improvement and discover a small bud of confidence, though I had no illusions about achieving dolphin-like proficiency by the end of the course. Gradually I reached the stage of putting together all the various body movements and the breathing to produce my highly personalised version of the crawl while we also tried a bit of breast stroke and I learned to float on my back. Sometimes we were allowed to use flippers, which was a bit like strapping on an outboard motor; when the flippers had to come off, though, it was back to the reality of being blessed with the aerodynamics and buoyancy of a house brick.

Before the start of September Maria and I had both faced the daunting prospect of handing in our resignations. It was a genuinely hard thing to do not only because we enjoyed our respective work places but also because everyone had been so good to us and we couldn't help feeling we were letting them down. Colleagues were sorry to see us go but were also very supportive and envious about our impending move to America and the adventures which lay ahead for us there. We enjoyed a touching round of farewell functions, the highlight being dinner at one of Brisbane's top Vietnamese restaurants attended by around 25 colleagues from the university. Maria also had a lunch at the university staff club, we both put on morning teas, there were speeches, goodbye gifts and final photos. And that was the end of work until we reached Boulder.

Our last few days in Brisbane were also characterised by the usual scramble associated with leaving one country for another—tying up numerous loose ends and making endless lists. We had to clean the flat, reclaim our bond, pay all the bills, and then close our bank account. We also had to slog through a couple of tax returns. We'd not long finished the one for New Zealand and now had to whip off the Aussie forms which were due by the end of October. There is a great scheme in Australia whereby you can pay $20 to file your tax return through the post office on an express route that delivers refunds in as little as 10 days. Since we were in the fortunate position of having some money due back we took this option and even had all our tax affairs up to date by the day we left. There is no doubt the whole tax system is generally much more user-friendly and the forms much simpler in New Zealand and Australia. In England and America filing tax returns is a nightmare. The tax packs, each containing a small plantation of pulped conifers, should come stamped in red: "Warning: Don't try this at home." The trouble is, as we discovered in the States, even when a qualified accountant takes over the job it's no guarantee of plain sailing.

We spent our last evening in Brisbane shopping for a new suitcase. We had already bought one extra bag, filled it with clothes and watched it burst open as soon as we tried to pick it up. So out we went to buy something a bit more solid. It only had to last as far as New Zealand as a lot of what we were carting back was going straight to our daughter's flat in Christchurch. We slept that final night at the youth hostel where the Brisbane chapter of our travels had all started almost a year before. The next morning we crossed the Tasman, still on different flights but this time only 10 minutes apart. I caught up with Maria at the baggage claim area of Christchurch airport.

It was only four months since we'd been in New Zealand and while it was great to be back we didn't have the same nerve-tingling sense of excitement as previously. Also it was bloody cold in Christchurch, especially after Brisbane, and I immediately caught an annoying chill that blighted the start of this holiday. We spent the first few days in Christchurch, shopping and socialising with Emma and her boyfriend, and the last few days in Wellington where William was now working in a very trendy cafe called The Globe. Emma joined us there, bringing with her three continuous days of rain which sent us scuttling into shops, cinemas, museums and, of course, the friendly, welcoming Globe. Sandwiched in between these two cities was another of our famous, frantic, fleeting visits to Blenheim.

We had allowed ourselves just six days and, as usual, had lots to do. We still had not booked our onward flight to America so that loomed large on our "to do" list. We considered all sorts of travel options but ruled out another round-the-world ticket; since we expected to be in the States the best part of a year there was no way we would be able to make full use of such a flexible ticket. Instead we tracked down a good deal through Air New Zealand which would take us to Europe in a year's time. We bought one-way tickets to Germany, travelling via the States, with a final onward leg from Frankfurt to Paris. We were already looking 12 months ahead to a holiday in France before arriving in England for another stint of Animal Aunts.

We were to fly out of Wellington for Los Angeles on October 11. But before then there was the small matter of sorting out insurance for the coming year. Up to this point insurance had not been an issue; our belongings were barely worth insuring and, since we had been spending most of our time in the UK and Australia, reciprocal arrangements between those countries and New Zealand gave us at least a minimum of health and medical cover. But all that was about to change...as everyone knows, setting foot in the USA without water-tight medical cover is just asking for a 10-ton weight to drop on your head.

Adequate cover was going to cost well over $1,000 in New Zealand but then we had the good fortune to find out we could get the same thing, and more, for just $60 each. All we had to do was take out Gold Mastercards and with them came a year's overseas insurance. Brilliant. Not only that but every time we used the cards—and we did tend to use them a lot—we earned air points. The first sizeable chunk of points landed almost immediately when we whipped out the cards to pay for our tickets. It was a fantastic deal all round...a little too good, in fact. A year later the credit card company stopped being so generous and introduced much more restrictive rules: the insurance still covered trips abroad but not for people like us living and working overseas.

At the first opportunity we went round to our house, dived into the front room and began fossicking for our ski gear and other winter woollies. Although it was several years since we'd been skiing we were looking forward to being back in the thick of it in one of the world's major ski areas. At the same time Colorado offered the faintly daunting prospect of our first winter for more than two years. By this stage we had also lashed out on other essentials—two *Lonely Planet* guide books, one on Colorado, the other on the American south west, and a large scale road map of middle and south western USA.

Naturally we spent time with Buffy who seemed remarkably sprightly for his 13 years, managed a couple of therapeutic hours hacking away at the undergrowth in our garden, and lapped up the hot news that the long-established, family-owned newspaper where I used to work had just been bought by one of the country's major media empires. But the highlight of this visit was undoubtedly a party organised weeks before we arrived to celebrate our 25th wedding anniversary. Quite a crowd of us piled into a seafood restaurant at Havelock, a little township a few miles outside Blenheim, where a good time was had by all. Even a handful of strangers, who happened to choose that night to dine out, acquitted themselves well during the inter-table singing competitions.

It was amazing to think we had been married a quarter of a century and in some ways it was a bitter-sweet celebration for us. Looking around the restaurant that night there were not many couples so fortunate. A high proportion of our friends and acquaintances had divorced and were now either single or remarried. We had also recently been forcefully reminded how lucky we were with our continuing good health. Two people we knew well needed urgent heart surgery while three other friends were struck by cancer: one didn't make it, the other two recovered after enduring terribly debilitating chemotherapy and radiation therapy. Things like that inevitably make you pause and take stock. It certainly gave us a renewed appreciation of our own good fortune and reinforced our determination to carry on with this gypsy lifestyle for as long as we kept enjoying it.

0-595-22668-X

Printed in the United States
20611LVS00007B/139-204

9 780595 226689